Fun with Nature

Fun with Nature

DOVER PUBLICATIONS, INC.
MINEOLA, NEW YORK

education.com

Copyright

Bibliographical Note

Fun with Nature, first published by Dover Publications, Inc., in 2015, contains pages from the following online workbooks published by Education.com: *Drawing Conclusions, Natural Resources, Can You Dig It? Rocks and Soil,* and *Tree-mendous Trees.*

International Standard Book Number

ISBN-13: 978-0-486-80265-7
ISBN-10: 0-486-80265-5

Manufactured in the United States by Courier Corporation
80265501 2015
www.doverpublications.com

CONTENTS

Drawing Conclusions

Insect Parts

What are the parts that make up an insect?
Using the words below, fill in the name of the part in the label.

stinger abdomen compound eyes head wings thorax legs mandible antennae

Parts of a Tree

What are the parts that make up a tree? Use the word bank below to help you research and remember all the parts of a tree. Then write the names in the labels. Hints are there to help you.

word bank

- primary root
- outer bark
- crown
- secondary roots
- inner bark
- heartwood
- trunk

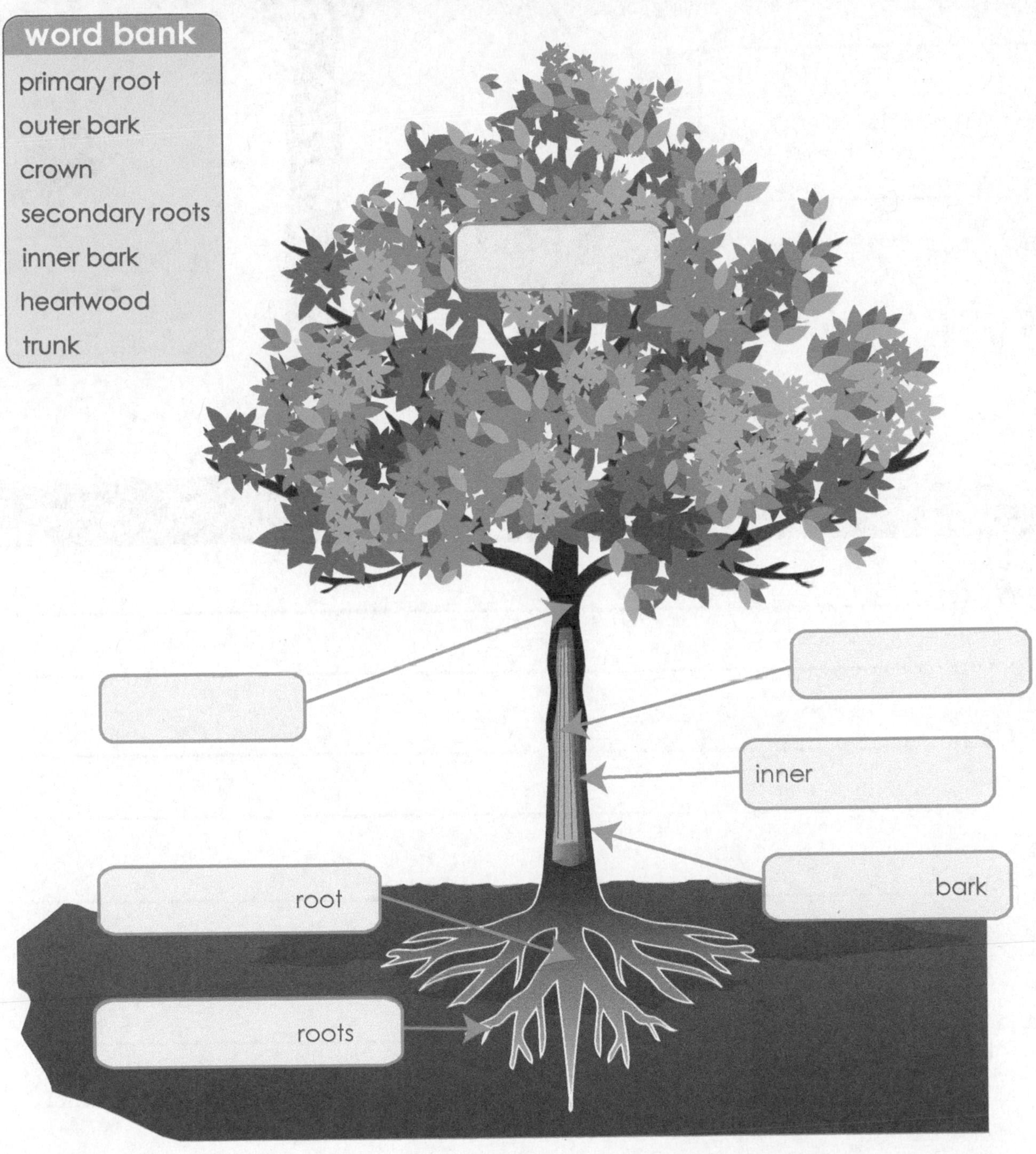

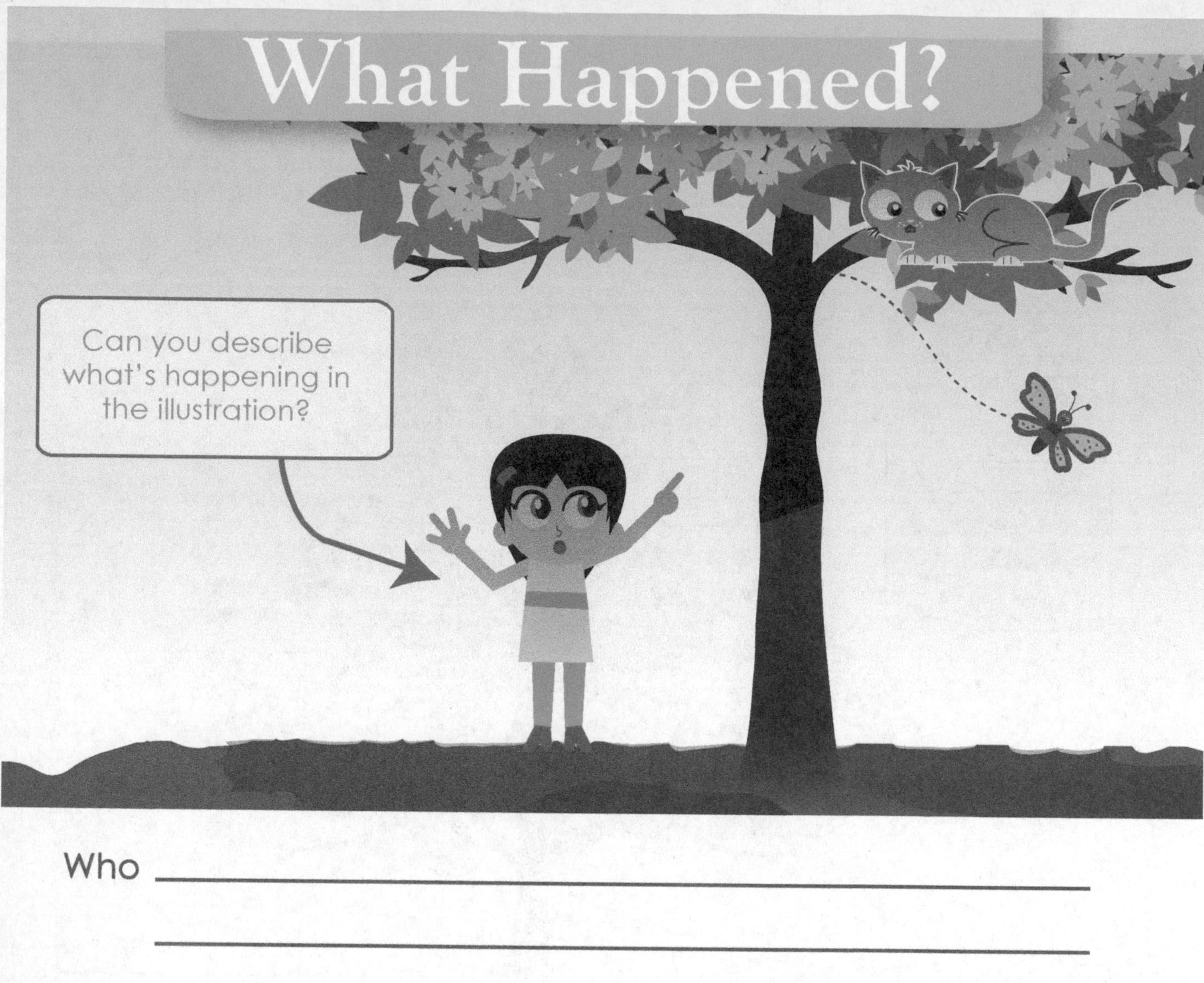

What Happened?
Can you describe what's happening in the illustration?

Who ____

____

What ____

____

Where ____

____

When ____

____

What Happened?

By using the information given in the "**why**" and "**how**," draw a picture of the kitten before it got stuck in the tree.

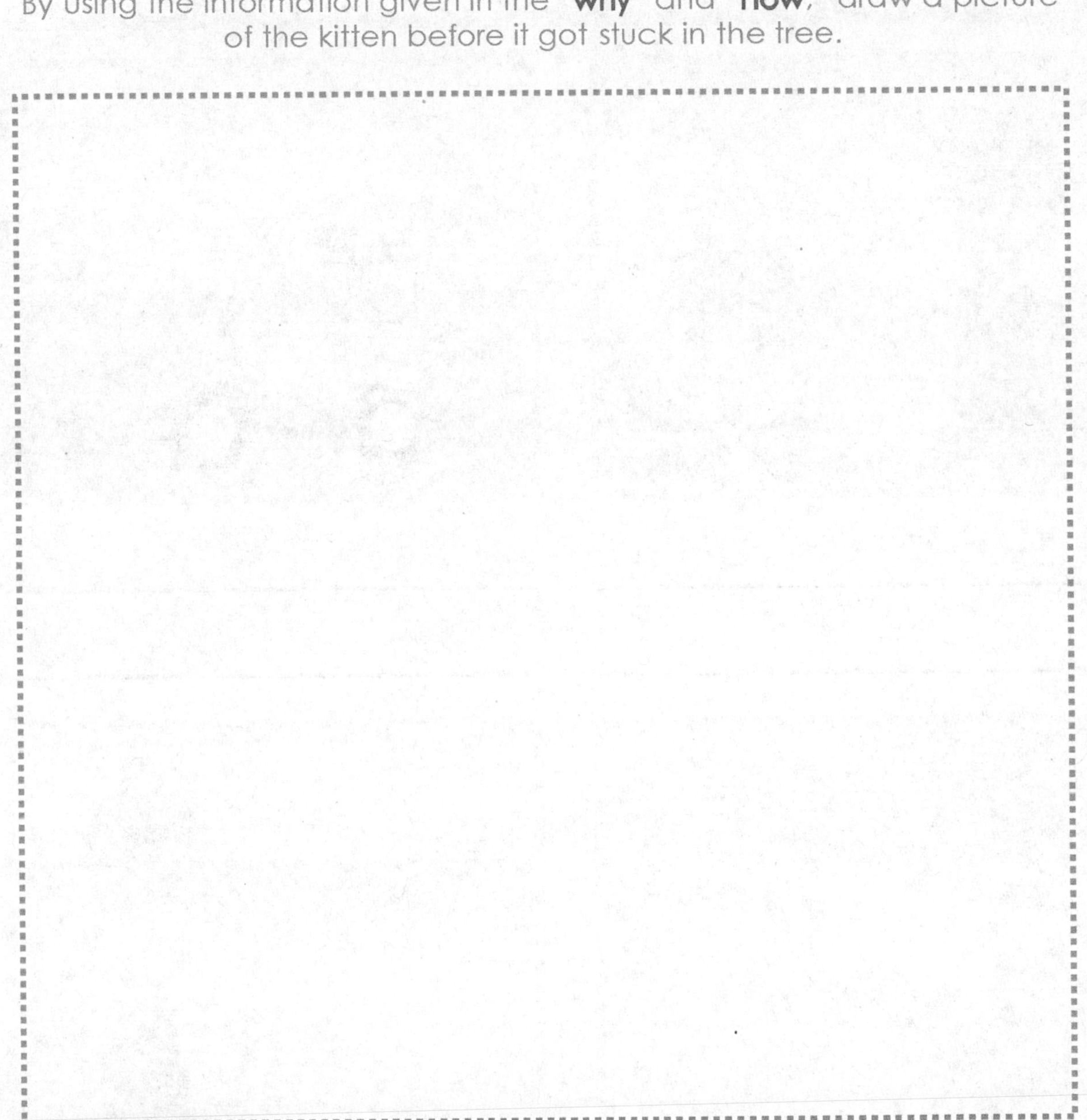

Why: The kitten saw a big, colorful butterfly and wanted to chase it!

How: The gate was left open, so the kitten got out and chased the butterfly up the tree.

Chuck's Vacation

Look at each photograph, and write a caption for each picture. Each caption should describe what you see in the photograph.

Chuck's Vacation

Look at each photograph, and write a caption for each picture. Each caption should describe what you see in the photograph.

Rooms in a House

What are the parts that make up a house? Use the words below to help you remember all the rooms in a house. Then write the names in the labels.

living room	dining room	bathroom	office	kitchen	bedroom	yard

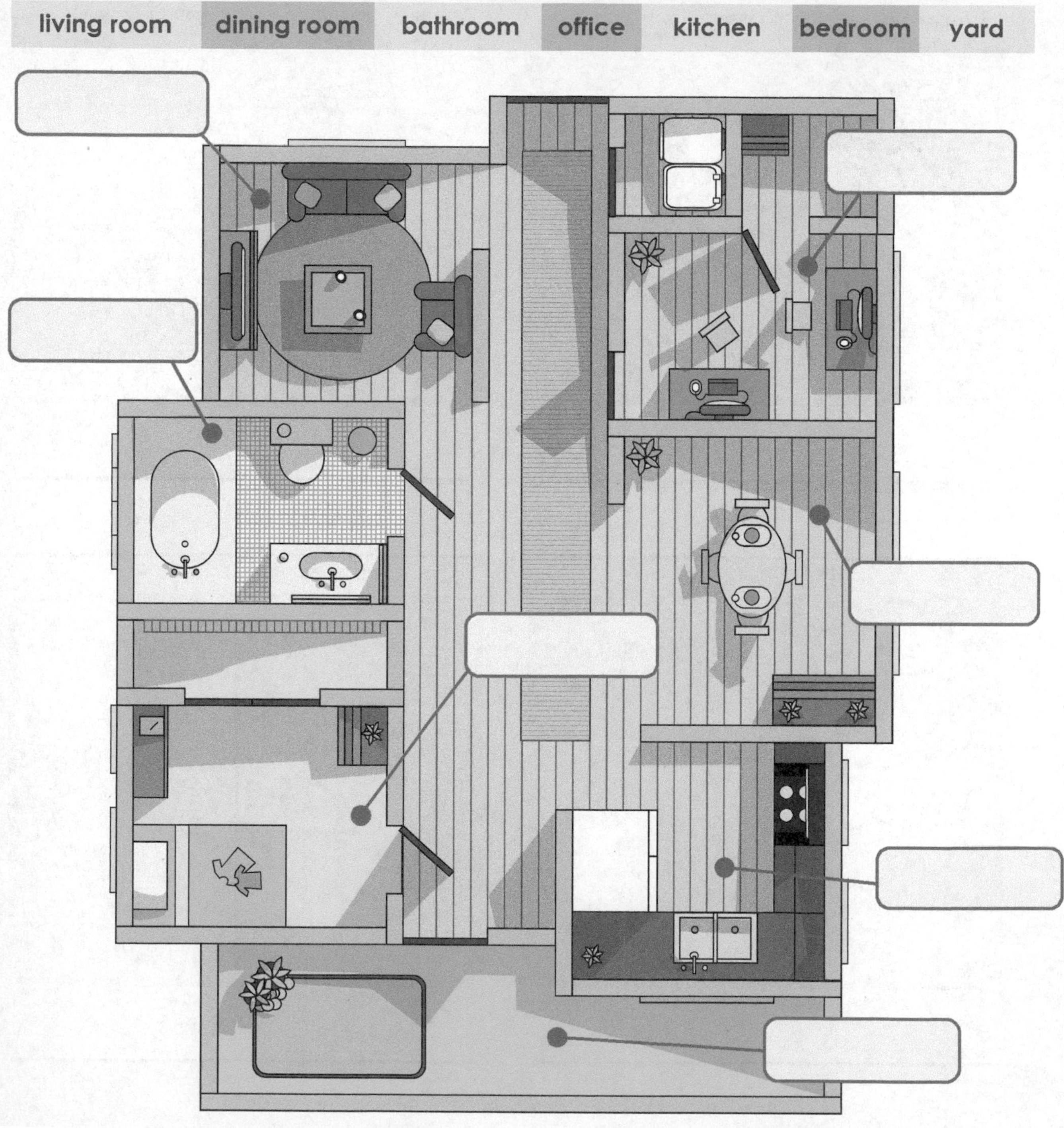

Parts of a Classroom

What are the parts that make up a classroom? Use the words below to help you remember all the parts in a classroom. Then fill in the labels.

teacher's desk	whiteboard	student's desk	bookcase	computers	chalkboard

Using Venn Diagrams

Use the observations from page 11 to fill in the Venn diagram.

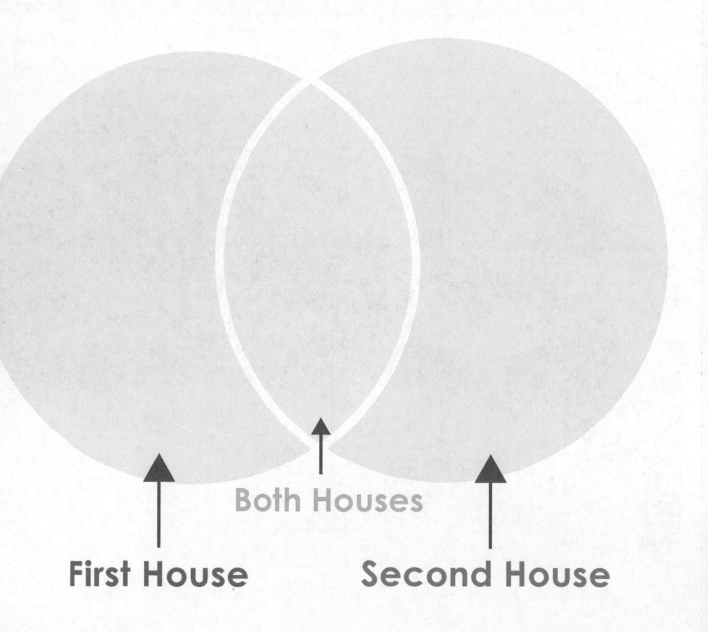

Both Houses

First House

Second House

Using Venn Diagrams

List the similarities and differences between these houses.

Similarities

1. ______
2. ______
3. ______
4. ______
5. ______
6. ______
7. ______
8. ______
9. ______
10. ______

Differences

1. ______
2. ______
3. ______
4. ______
5. ______
6. ______
7. ______
8. ______
9. ______
10. ______

LONG AGO versus TODAY VENN DIAGRAM

Use the Venn Diagram to see which items were used LONG AGO and / or TODAY.

DIRECTIONS: DRAW OR WRITE items from the past into the Long Ago circle and items used now in the Today circle. If they are used in both times, DRAW/WRITE them in the overlap in the middle. An example would be the book!

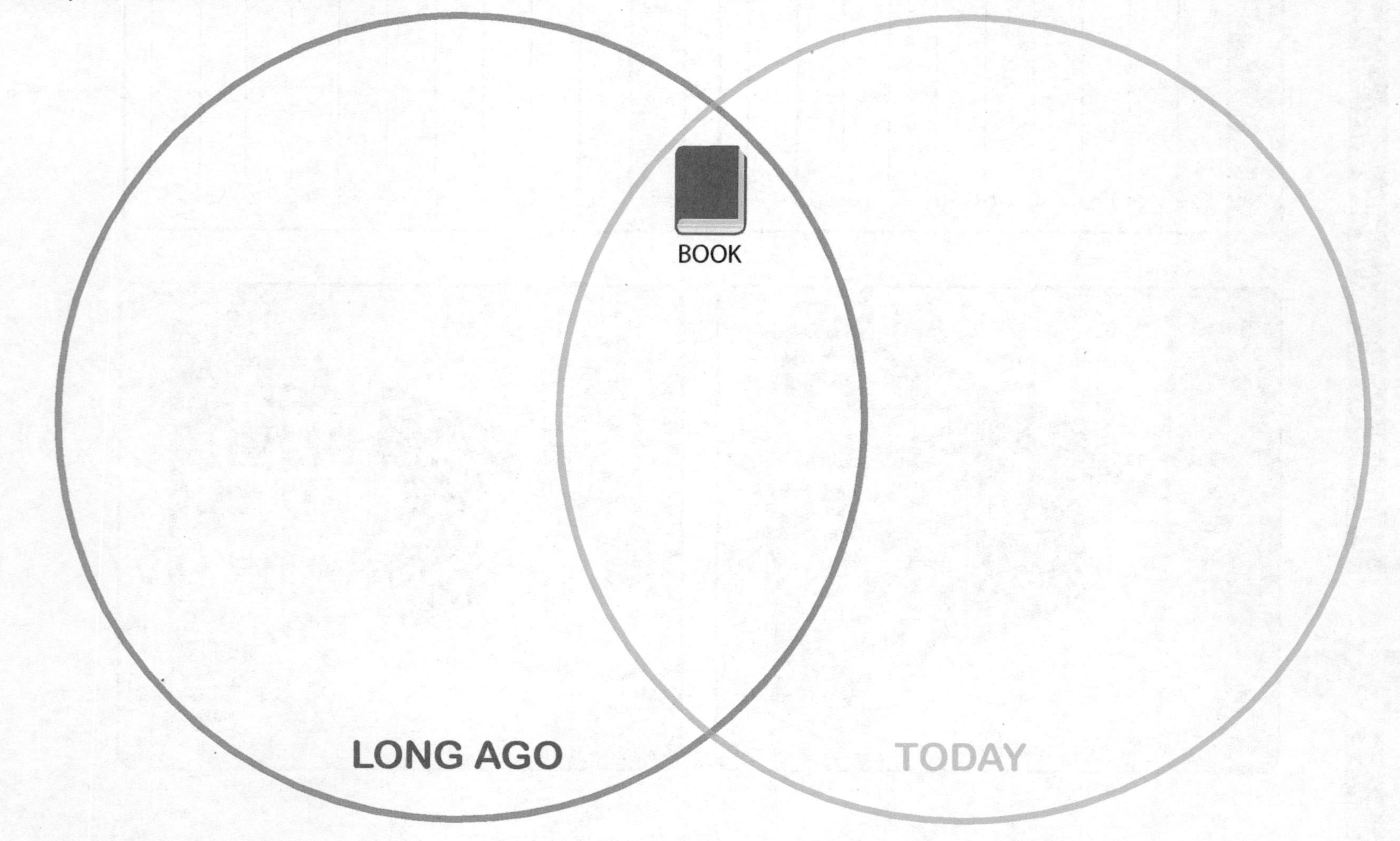

LONG AGO versus TODAY VENN DIAGRAM

Use the Venn Diagram to see which items were used LONG AGO and / or TODAY

DIRECTIONS:

Cut and paste the items below. Paste items from the past into the Long Ago circle and items used now in the Today circle. If they are used in both times, put them in the overlap in the middle. An example would be the book!

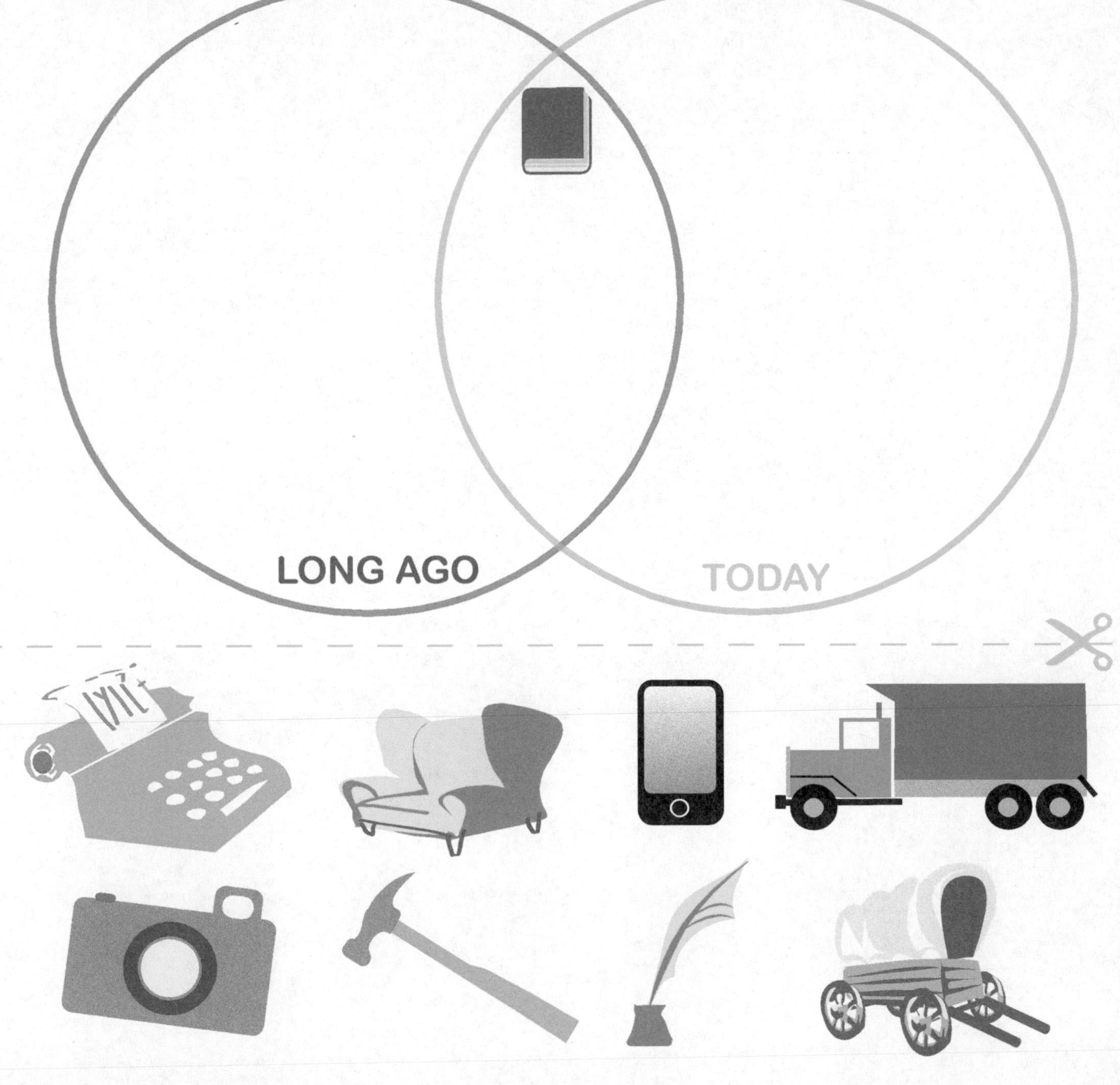

Soil, Sand, or Dirt?

Where can you find soil, sand, and dirt?

Write in the space provided under each picture.

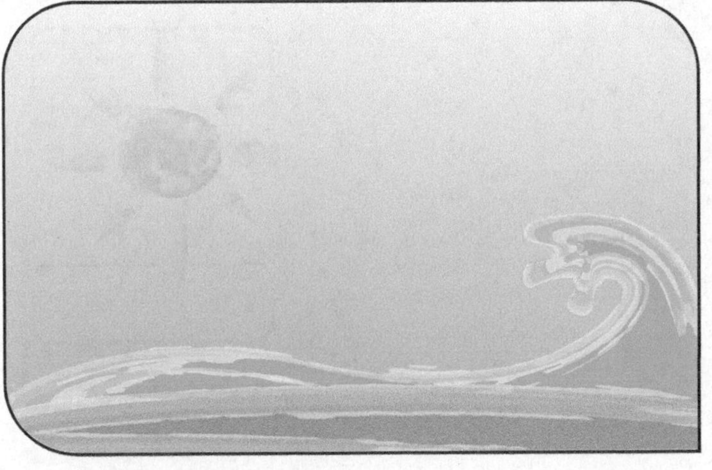

Soil

Is what the outside of the earth is made of.

Sand

Is made from tiny pieces of rocks and minerals.

Dirt

Is soil or sand that has been taken out of its natural environment.

How Do Clouds Form?

Use the words below and clues at the bottom to fill in the labels that describe how a cloud is formed.

heat cool liquid water rise cloud

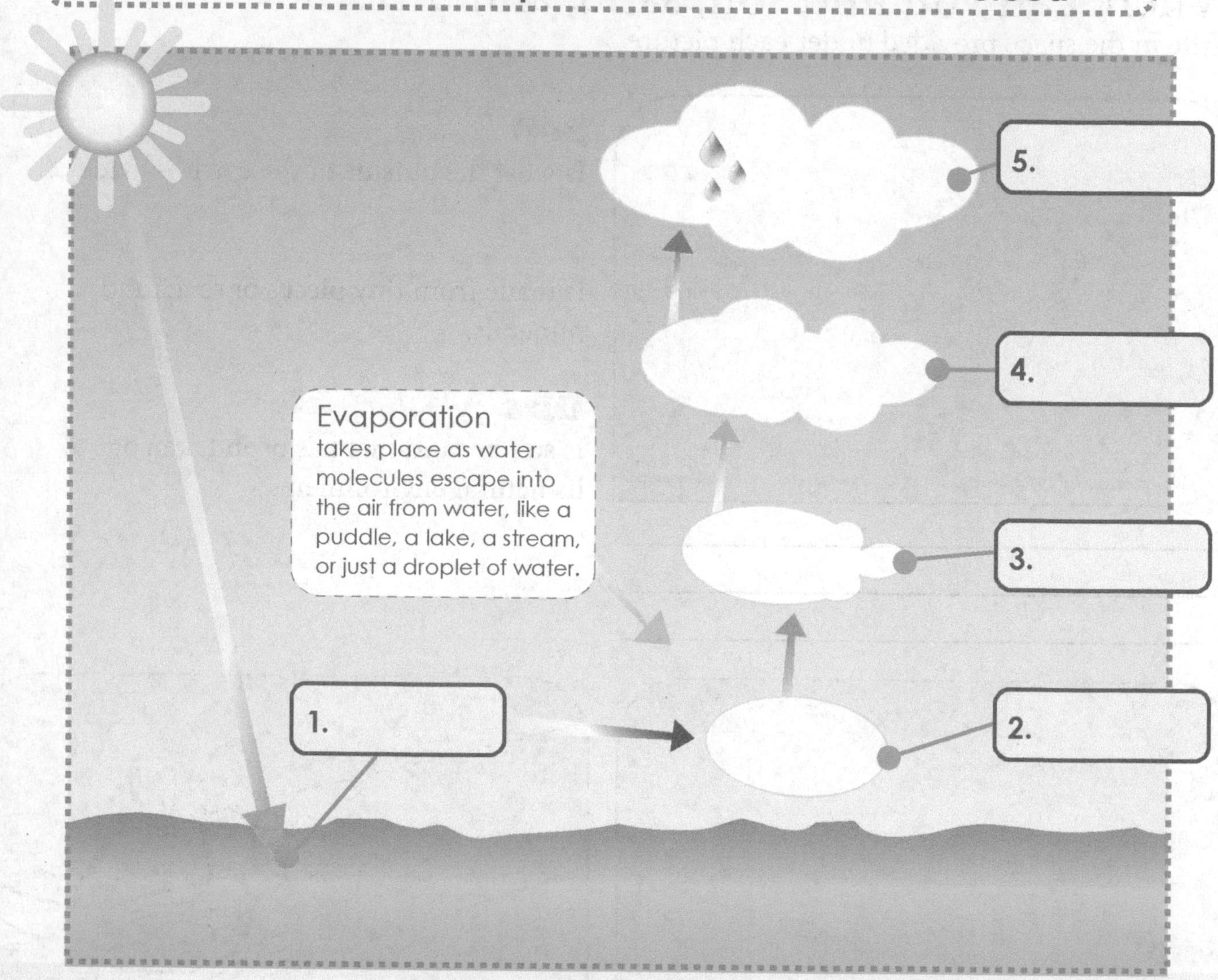

5.

4.

Evaporation
takes place as water molecules escape into the air from water, like a puddle, a lake, a stream, or just a droplet of water.

3.

1.

2.

1. Rays of the sun ________________ up the moisture in the air close to the ground.
2. As these pockets of air are heated they begin to ____________________.
3. As these heated pockets of air rise they____________________________.
4. As they cool, the water vapor turns to tiny droplets of ___________________.
5. The droplets crowd together and form a ____________________________.

The Water Cycle

Use the clues at the bottom to draw in the icons needed to finish the water cycle

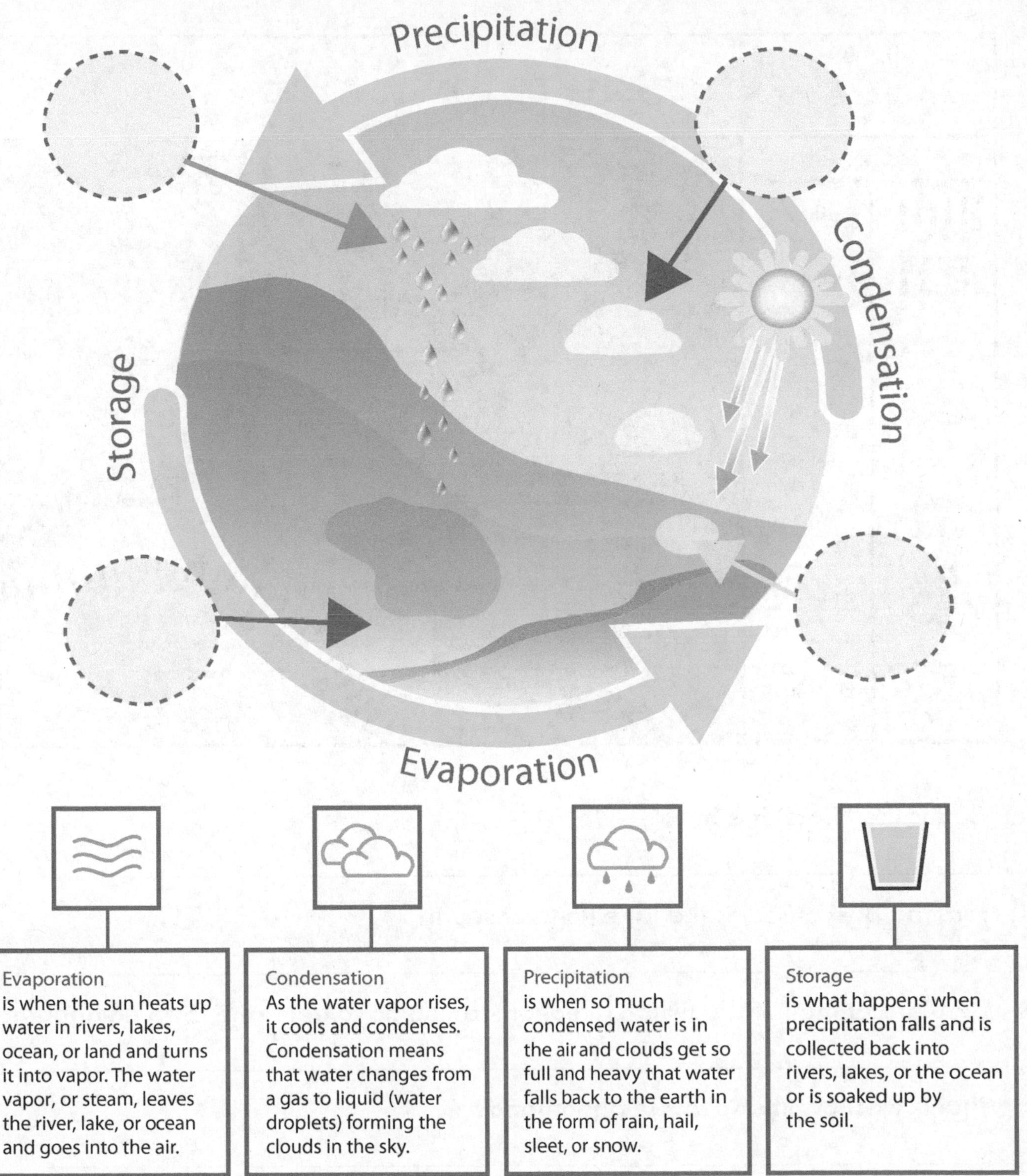

Evaporation	Condensation	Precipitation	Storage
Evaporation is when the sun heats up water in rivers, lakes, ocean, or land and turns it into vapor. The water vapor, or steam, leaves the river, lake, or ocean and goes into the air.	Condensation As the water vapor rises, it cools and condenses. Condensation means that water changes from a gas to liquid (water droplets) forming the clouds in the sky.	Precipitation is when so much condensed water is in the air and clouds get so full and heavy that water falls back to the earth in the form of rain, hail, sleet, or snow.	Storage is what happens when precipitation falls and is collected back into rivers, lakes, or the ocean or is soaked up by the soil.

Reading a Map

Study the map and use it to answer the questions below.

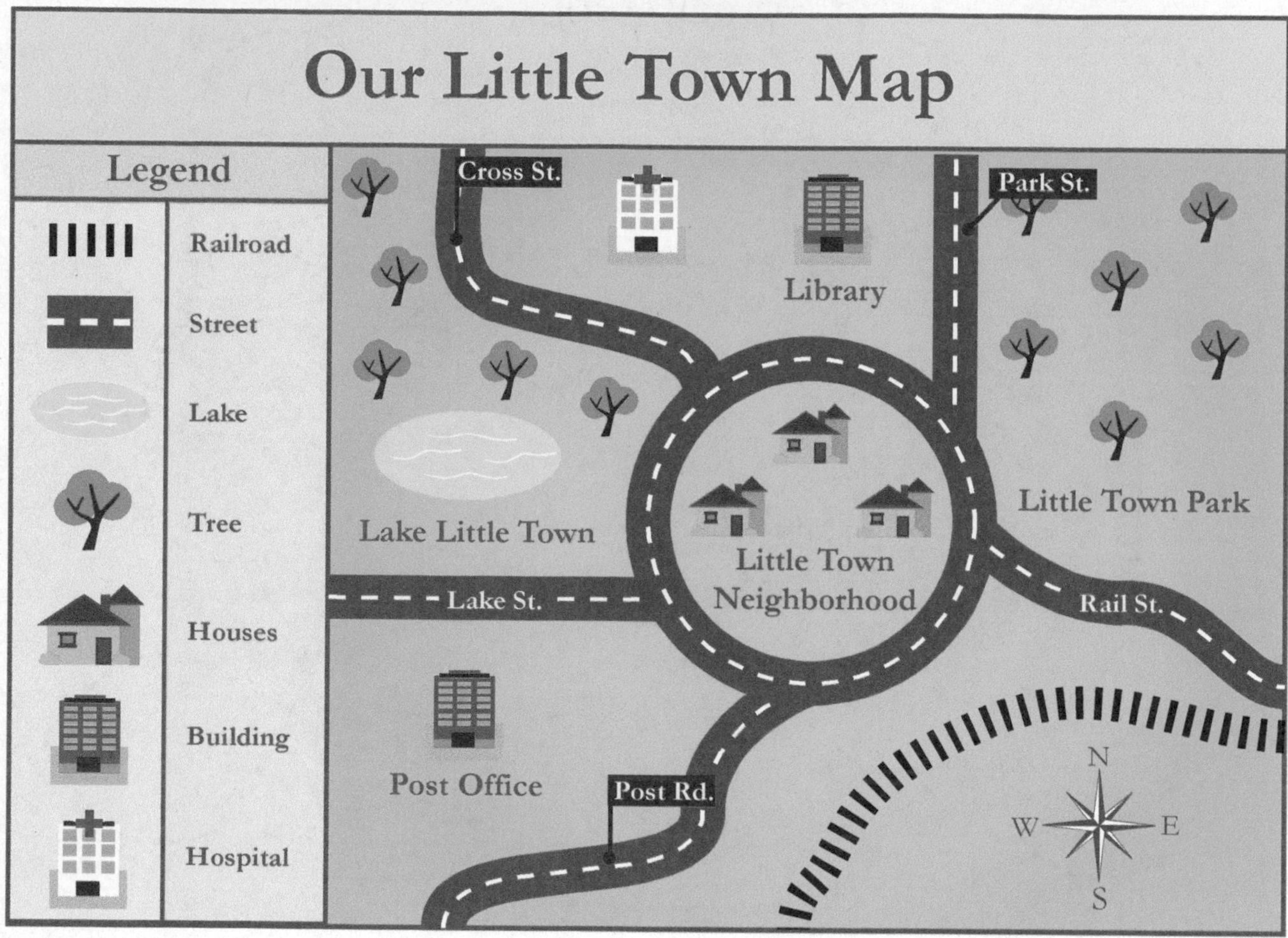

1. What is the title of this map?

____

2. From the post office, is the lake north or south?

____

3. If you are at the library, which direction do you go to get tothe town neighborhood?

____

4. What is west of Little Town Neighborhood?

____

5. What building is east of the hospital?

____

WORLD MAP

DIRECTIONS:

1. Draw and label the Prime Meridian in PURPLE. Draw and label the Equator in ORANGE.
2. Fill in the compass rose with the cardinal directions.
3. Color the oceans BLUE and label all five oceans.
4. Color & label the continents. Color North America RED. Color South America ORANGE. Color Europe PURPLE. Color Africa YELLOW. Color Asia GREEN. Color Australia BROWN. Color Antarctica GREY.

WORD BOX

EQUATOR
PRIME MERIDIAN
NORTH AMERICA
SOUTH AMERICA
AUSTRALIA
AFRICA
ASIA
ANTARCTICA
EUROPE
PACIFIC OCEAN
ATLANTIC OCEAN
INDIAN OCEAN
SOUTHERN OCEAN
ARCTIC OCEAN
NORTH
SOUTH
EAST
WEST

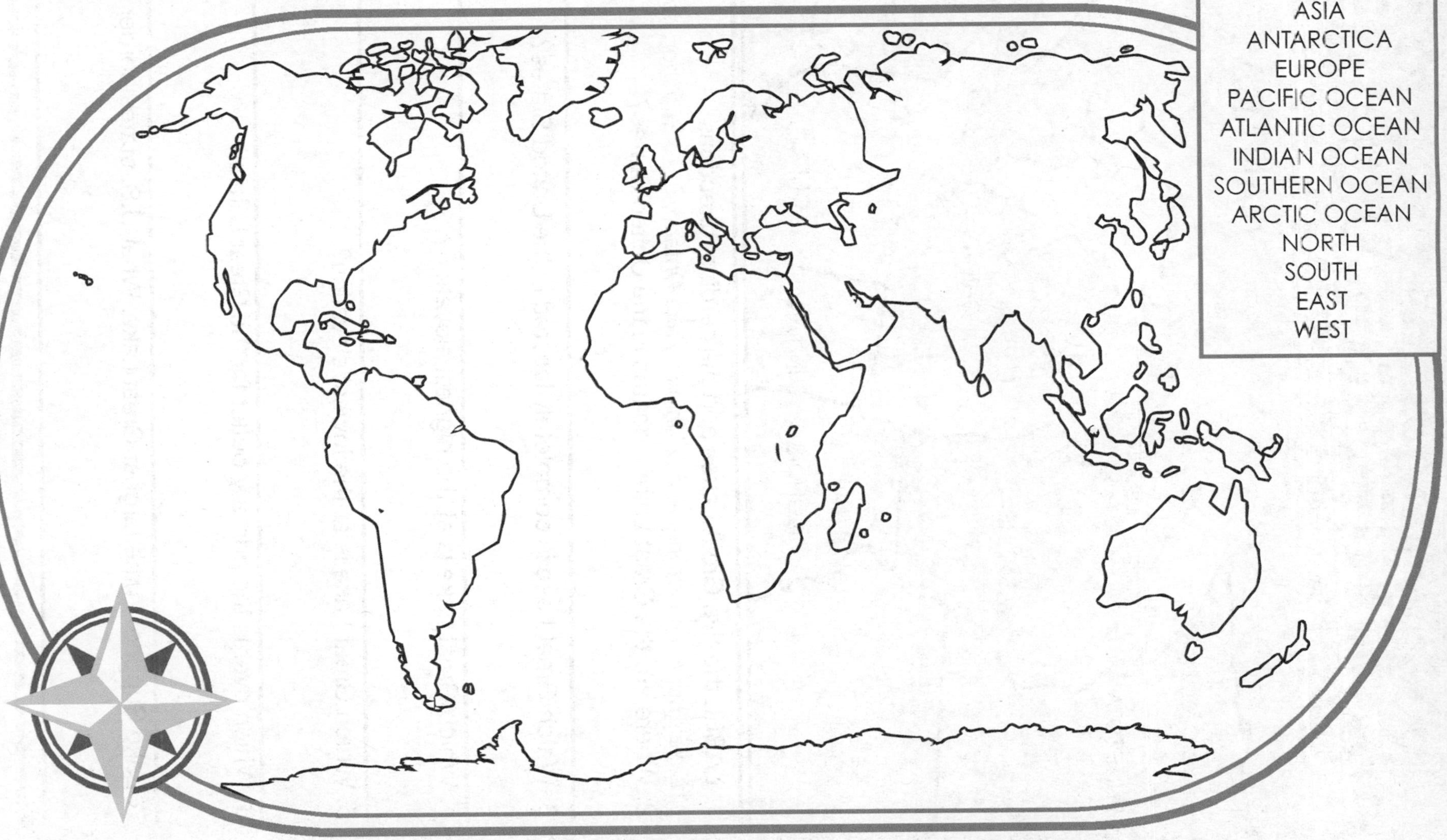

THE GREAT LAKES

1. LABEL the five Great Lakes and the cardinal directions.
   Lake Erie, Lake Huron, Lake Michigan, Lake Ontario, Lake Superior, north, east, south, west
2. Where are the Great Lakes located in the United States?

   ____
3. Which Great Lake is completely located in the United States?

   ____
4. Which Great Lake is at the highest elevation?

   ____
5. Which Great Lake is at the lowest elevation?

   ____
6. Which river is the primary outlet for the Great Lakes?

   ____
7. Lake Superior is the largest Great Lake. What U.S. states border Lake Superior?

   ____

Major U.S. Rivers

Do you know the major rivers of the United States? Use the words below and clues at the bottom to fill in the labels.

Missouri **Mississippi** **Colorado** **Rio Grande** **Hudson** **Ohio**

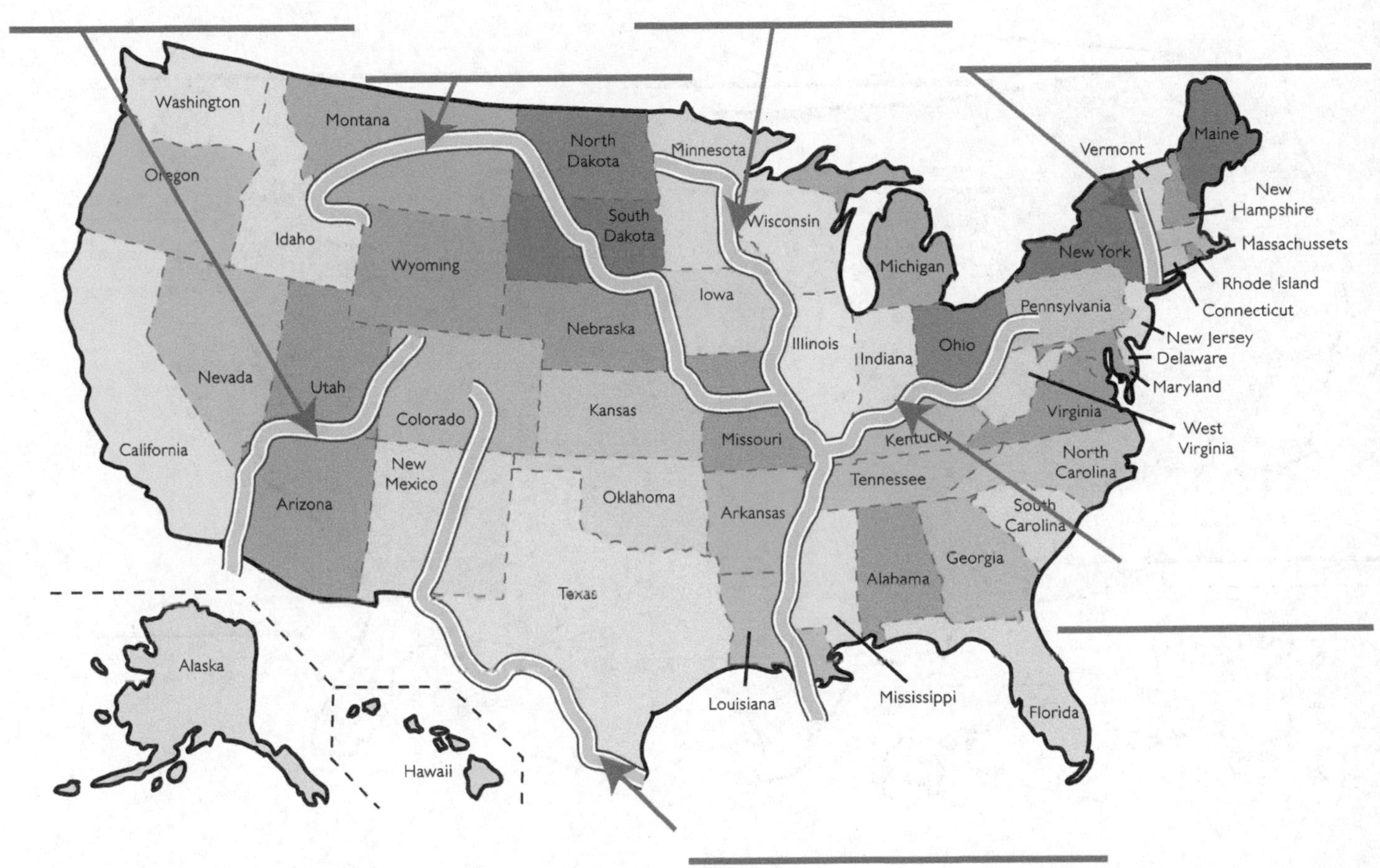

1. This is the major river of the U.S. It flows south from Minnesota and empties into the Gulf of Mexico.
2. This river flows into the Mississippi. It forms part of the borders of Ohio, West Virginia, and more.
3. This river begins in Colorado, flows through New Mexico, and then along the border of Texas.
4. This river begins in Colorado. It moves southwest, ending in the Gulf of California.
5. This river begins in New York, then flows south to form the boundary with New Jersey.
6. This river begins in Montana and flows southeast across the U.S. It ends at the Mississppi River.

Major U.S. Mountains

Do you know the major mountain ranges of the United States?
Use the words below and clues at the bottom to fill in the labels.

Rocky Mountains **Central Appalachians** **Cascade Mountains**
Sierra Nevada Mountains **Northern Appalachians**

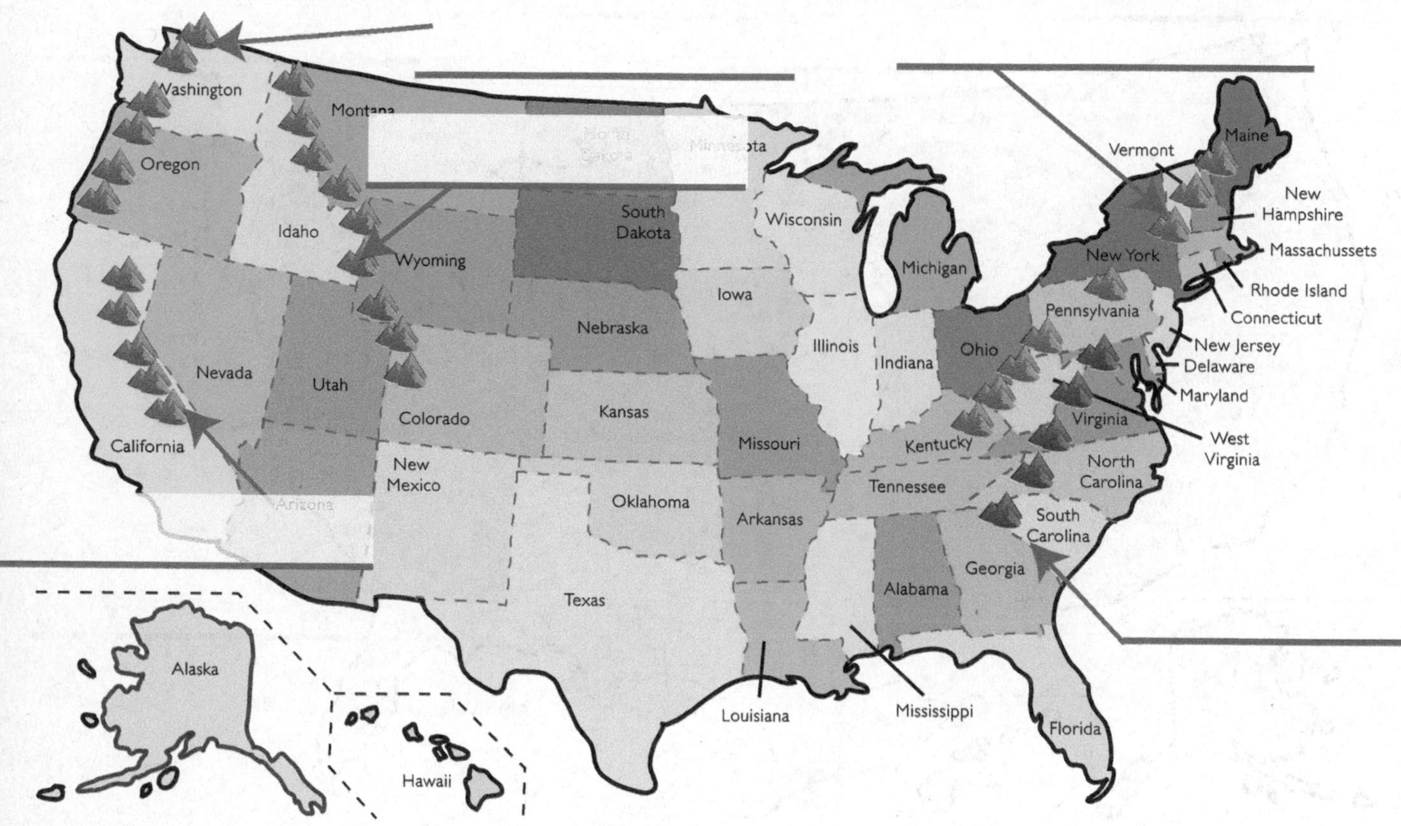

1. These mountains go from Canada to the western U.S. Yellowstone Park is part of this range.
2. This is a sub-section of a larger range; it goes from Canada to the northeastern U.S.
3. This range is full of glaciers and volcanoes, and stretches from Northern California to Canada.
4. This range of snowy mountains is in California and Nevada. Lake Tahoe is in this range.
5. This is a sub-section of a larger range; it goes from Georgia to Pennsylvania.

Great job!
is an Education.com reading superstar

Natural Resources

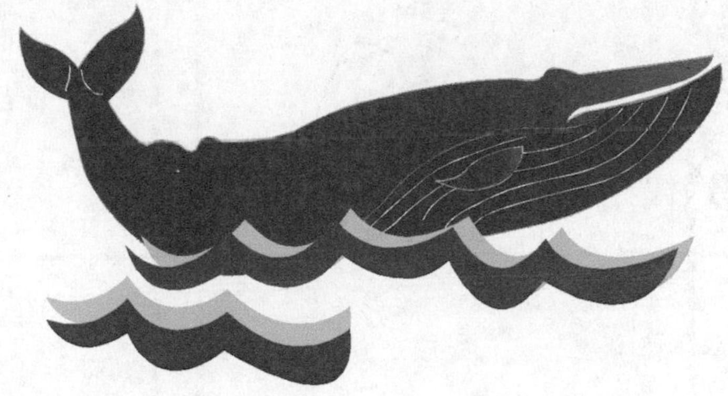

RESOURCES

There are 3 main types of Resources. DRAW FOUR ITEMS UNDER EACH.
HUMAN RESOURCES are people who use their skills to produce a good or service. (Ex. Teacher.)
NATURAL RESOURCES are from nature and are used in their natural form. (Ex. Trees.)
CAPITAL RESOURCES are goods produced and used to make other goods or services. (Ex. Buildings, Computers.)

CAPITAL RESOURCES	HUMAN RESOURCES	NATURAL RESOURCES
 VAN	 SCIENTIST	 SUN

RESOURCES

There are 3 main types of Resources. CUT and PASTE the images under the resource they match!

HUMAN RESOURCES are people who use their skills to produce a good or service. (Ex. Teacher.)

NATURAL RESOURCES are from nature and are used in their natural form. (Ex. Trees.)

CAPITAL RESOURCES are goods produced and used to make other goods or services. (Ex. Buildings, Computers.)

CAPITAL RESOURCES	HUMAN RESOURCES	NATURAL RESOURCES

ROCK RESOURCES

Rocks are natural resources that people use to make things. Below are some examples. Draw more examples and write a description of each drawing in the space provided.

DIAMOND

PYRAMIDS

FIREPLACE

STEPS IN A GARDEN

MINERAL RESOURCES

Rocks are made of minerals and we use minerals in many ways.

For example, *iron* is a mineral resource that has to be mined from the ground. People use iron to make steel, which we then use to make all kinds of things such as the frames for skyscrapers, supports for bridges, and engines for cars.

Coal is another mineral resource that has to be mined from the ground. People use coal to make heat, which is necessary for comfortable living during winter, especially in very cold places like Canada and Alaska.

Below are four other mineral resources. Write two sentences for each that describes what these minerals are used for.

GOLD ______________________________

____

____

COPPER ______________________________

____

____

DIAMOND ______________________________

____

____

SALT ______________________________

____

____

WHAT GROWS AROUND US! PLANT RESOURCES

Plants are natural resources that people and animals use. Below are examples. Write down more examples and draw a picture of your favorite one.

Cotton plants provide material for clothing.

Bamboo provides flooring material for houses.

Flowers provide bees with nectar that they make into honey and we use honey to sweeten our food.

Trees are ground into pulp to make paper.

PETUNIA'S AND PETER'S PLANTS

Petunia and Peter like to use things that are made from plants. Cross out all of the items that do not come from plants. A little research might be in order!

Then put the remaining letters in order to spell out the answer to this riddle:

WHY ARE POTATOES GOOD DETECTIVES?

Because they ____eep ____he____r eyes ____ ____ ____ ____ ____ ____!

A BACON

F GLASS

C PLASTIC

I OATS

E TOFU

T PAPER

G MILK

L CORK

E RUBBER

P MAPLE SYRUP

E COTTON

D LUMBER

U CHEESE

K TEA

VENN DIAGRAM

Can you place products from the word bank below with the plant that produced it, or can be used to make it?

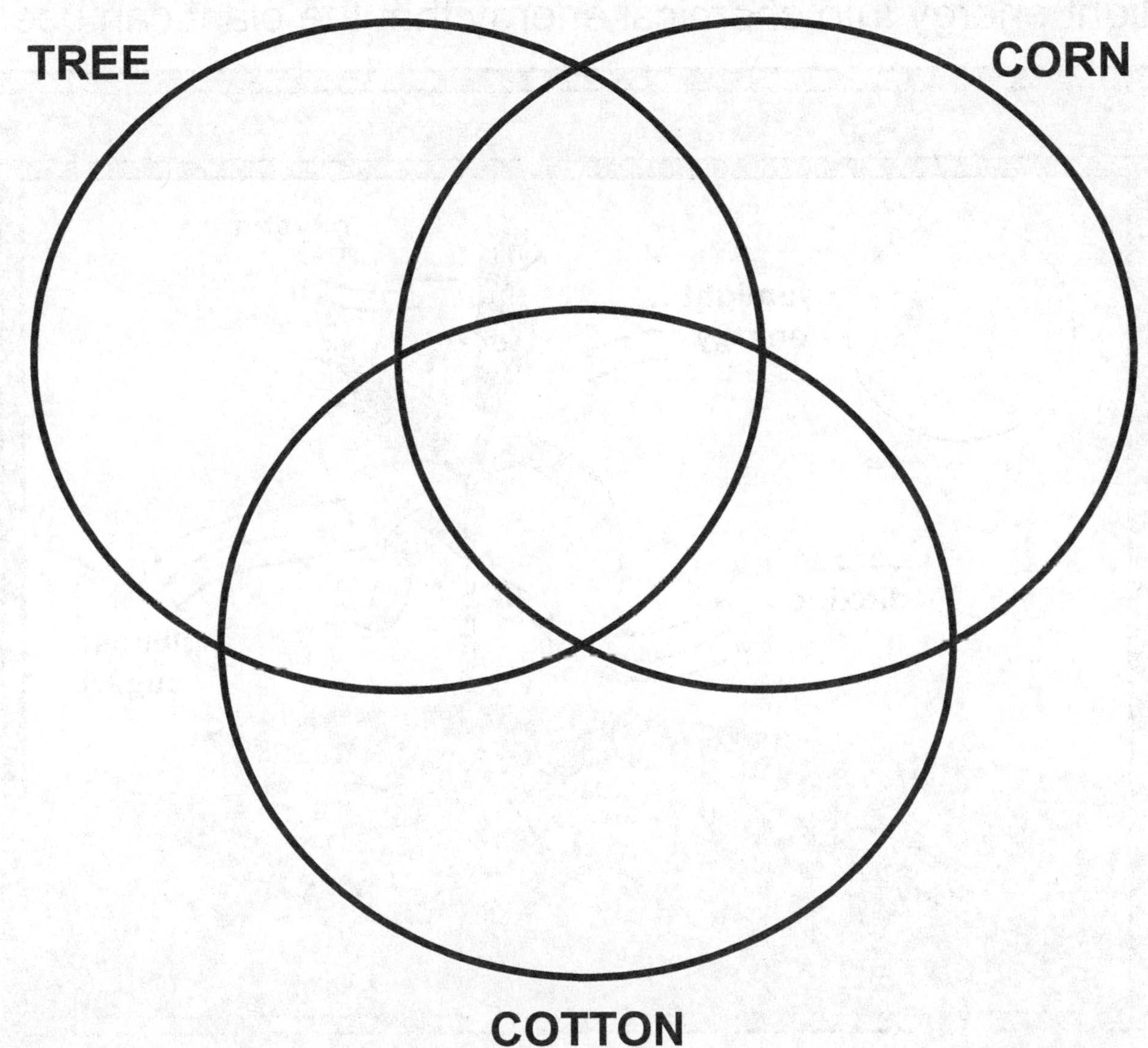

oxygen	**fuel**	**wood**	**clothes**
food for people	**particle board**	**feed for animals**	
furniture	**sweetener**	**paper**	

Photosynthesis

Plants are an important natural resource that are involved in the process of photosynthesis.
Photosynthesis is the process used by plants to convert light energy into chemical energy that the plant can use.

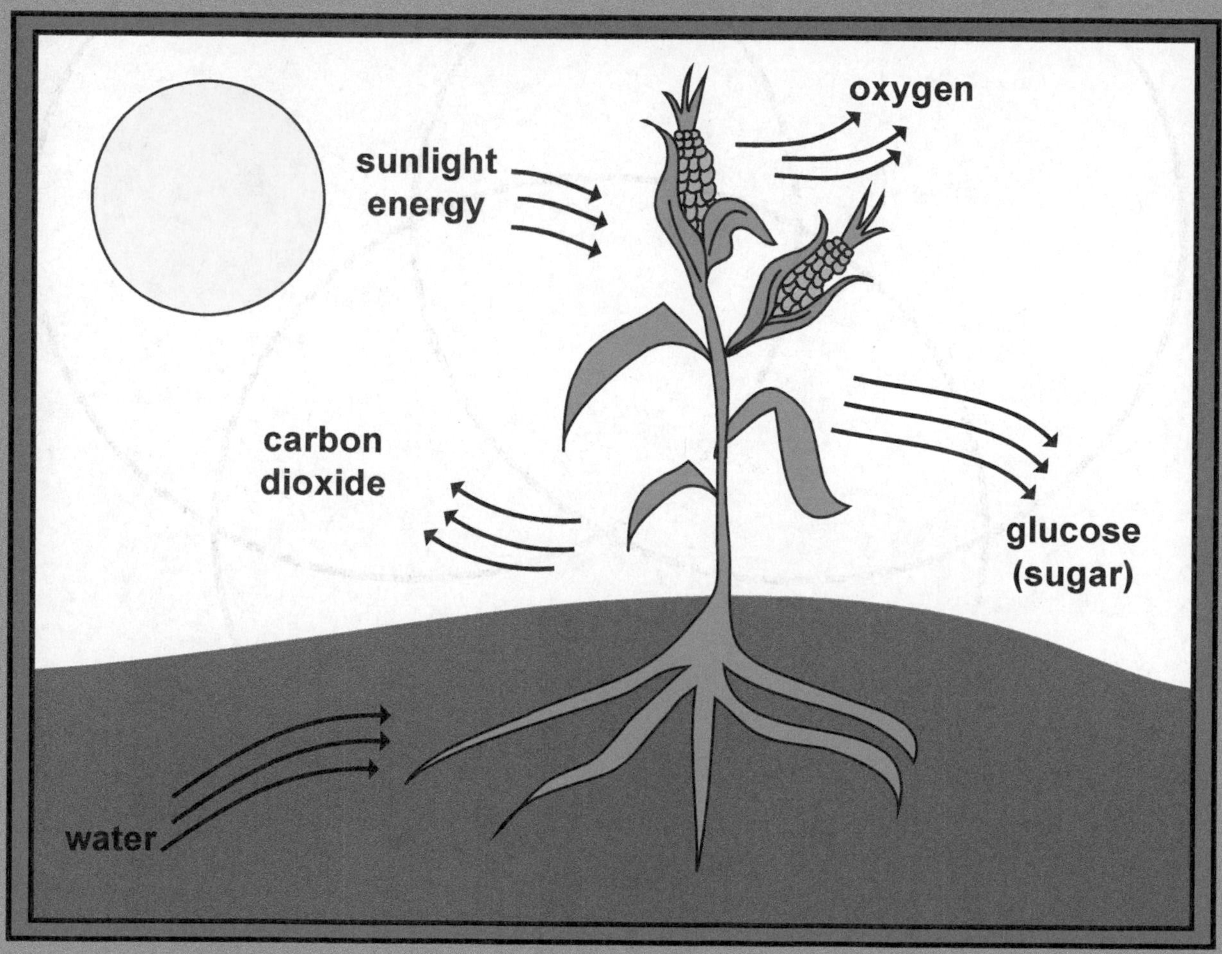

Plants provide people and animals with shelter, food, oxygen, and filtration to make the air clearer.

HIDDEN USES: BUILDING RESOURCES VOCABULARY

There are many kinds of natural resources. Some you know well, and some you don't know very well. Below on the left is a list of several natural resources you might not know very much about. On the right is a list of what these resources are used for. Draw a line from the resource on the left to the use of that resource on the right.

PETROLEUM (OIL) •	• FOOD
MARBLE •	• GASOLINE FOR POWERING CARS
NATURAL GAS •	• OBJECTS MADE OF GLASS
DIAMOND •	• DRILL BITS AND SAWS FOR CUTTING HARD OBJECTS
COPPER •	• HEATING HOMES
WOOD •	• OBJECTS MADE OF GLASS
SEAWEED •	• WIRES FOR CONDUCTING ELECTRICITY
SAND •	• FURNITURE

WHO EATS WHAT?

BUILDING RESOURCES VOCABULARY

Some animals, like tigers, are **carnivores**. That means they eat only meat (which comes from other animals).

Some animals, like deer, are **herbivores**, which means they eat only plants.

Human beings are called **omnivores**, because we eat plants and meat.

To continue building your resources vocabulary identify the animals below and on the next page as carnivores, herbivores, or omnivores.

____

RABBITS

____

EAGLES

GIANT PANDAS

RACCOONS

LEOPARDS

COWS

HAMSTERS

BEARS

COYOTES

SNAKES

SEA RESOURCES

The ocean is one of our greatest resources. The world's oceans provide many useful items and functions for not only people who live on the coast, but all people. The first thing that comes to mind when we think about sea resources is food, but the sea provides many other kinds of resources as well.

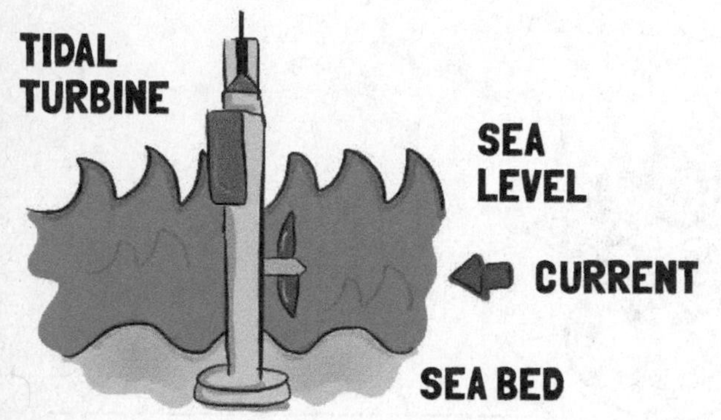

★ The world's oceans provide energy in the form of electricity from wave action. As waves crash on the beach they drive a turbine, a kind of engine, which produces electricity that we can use in our homes and buildings.

★ The world's oceans are providing water for people who live in dry places. This is mostly true in other countries where there isn't a lot of fresh water available. Salty sea water must have the salt removed before people can drink it. Huge machines in factories are necessary to make this happen. It's called *desalination*.

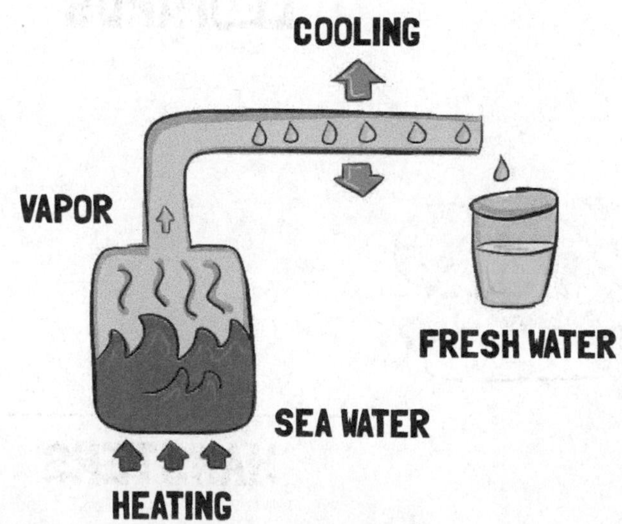

★ One of the most important ways we use the world's oceans and seas is transportation. It's not something we think about a lot, but it's true. Many of the products you use in your home—TVs, clothes, and even some kinds of food—were made elsewhere and shipped to the United States on large cargo vessels.

MORE IMPORTANT EVEN THAN TRANSPORTATION, HOWEVER, IS THE FOOD RESOURCE THAT THE SEAS PROVIDE. BELOW, LIST AT LEAST 10 KINDS OF FOOD THAT COMES FROM THE SEA:

1. ______________________________
2. ______________________________
3. ______________________________
4. ______________________________
5. ______________________________
6. ______________________________
7. ______________________________
8. ______________________________
9. ______________________________
10. ______________________________

WHAT'S YOUR FAVORITE SEAFOOD? DRAW IT BELOW.

RECREATIONAL RESOURCES

Most of the resources we talk about are needed for comfortable living and even survival. But there is another way to think about resources. There are the resources we use to have fun. These are called recreational resources.

Example: Many areas in the world are deserts that are very dry. Even though there isn't very much water in desert areas, people like to go there to have fun. For example, they drive dune buggies over the sand dunes.

BELOW IS A LIST OF SIX RECREATIONAL RESOURCES. WRITE ONE SENTENCE NEXT TO EACH ONE THAT DESCRIBES WHAT PEOPLE DO THERE TO HAVE FUN.

A beach where people can go into the water

____

____

____

____

A beach where people cannot go into the water

____

____

____

____

A forest

____

____

____

____

The mountains

A desert

A river

THE AIR WE BREATHE

The air we breathe is the most forgotten natural resource. It is invisible, but it is necessary for life on Earth!

Without the oxygen in the air, we wouldn't be able to survive. Air can't be used up or go away, but it can get dirty. In some cases, it can get so dirty that we can't use it to breath, or, using it can make us sick.

EXAMPLE

Factories that produce chemicals that go into the air can make the air unusable. One of the ways we can correct this and make the air a usable natural resource again is by making factories use filters that catch the chemicals before they can get into the environment.

BELOW IS A LIST OF FOUR WAYS THE RESOURCE OF AIR CAN BE RUINED. WRITE TWO SENTENCES THAT DESCRIBE HOW TO CORRECT THE PROBLEM.

1 **Cars produce chemicals in exhaust from running the engine that can ruin the air.**

2 **Pesticides and fertilizers used to grow large amounts of crops on large farms can ruin the air.**

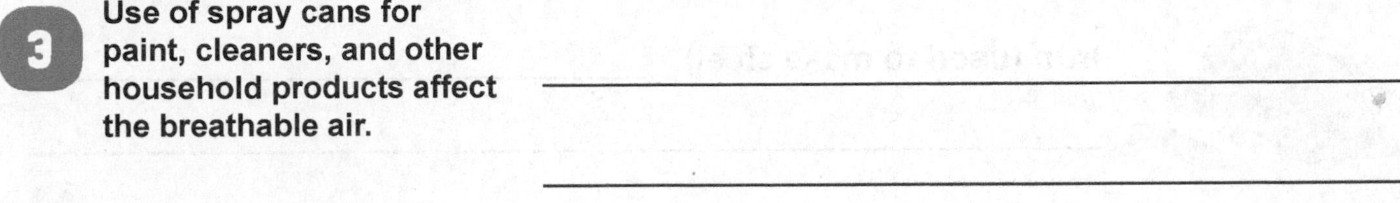

3 Use of spray cans for paint, cleaners, and other household products affect the breathable air.

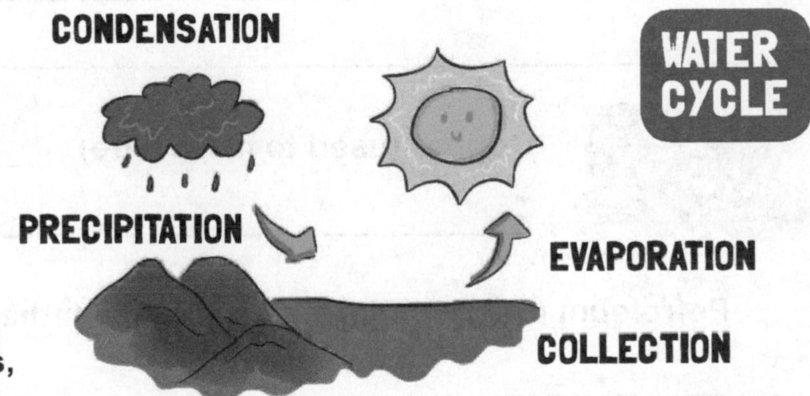

4 Chemicals get into the ocean from companies and factories, which contaminate rain water.

RESOURCES USED TO MAKE YOUR FAMILY CAR

Your family car is made of elements from a variety of natural resources.

For example, sand plays an important role in the production of glass. So, we can say the windows in your family car are made using the resource: sand.

Below is a list of four other natural resources used to make cars. Write two sentences that describe the part (or parts) of your car that is made from that resource:

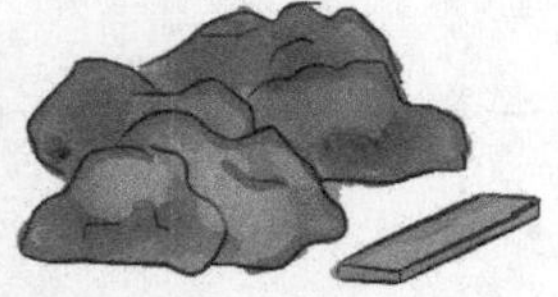

Iron (used to make steel) ______________________

____

Leather (from animals and used to cover seats in luxury cars)

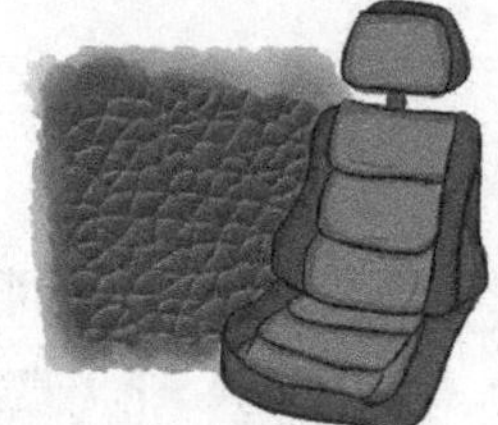

____

____

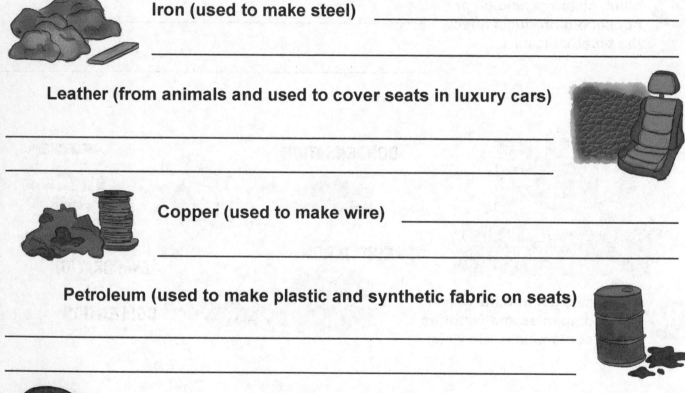

Copper (used to make wire) ______________________

____

Petroleum (used to make plastic and synthetic fabric on seats)

____

____

Rubber (from trees to make tires) ______________________

____

Leather (from animals and used to cover seats in luxury cars)

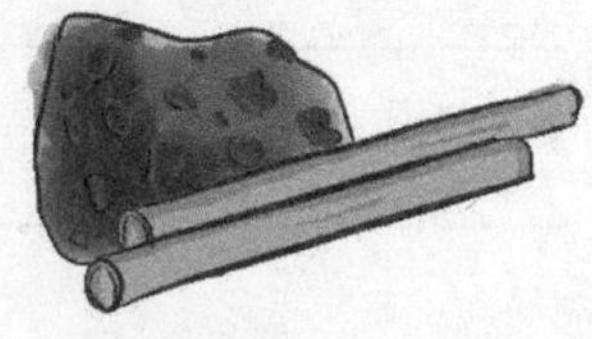

____

____

H2O (water that is necessary to help us turn iron ore into steel)

____

Natural Resources Mix and Match

Renewable resources are resources that can be replaced in a few years or decades, at about the same rate they are being used. Nonrenewable resources are resources that are being used up faster than they can be replaced. These resources can take anywhere from hundreds to millions of years to regenerate—and in some cases they never will.

Use the chart below to classify each resource as renewable or nonrenewable.

Renewable	Nonrenewable

NATURAL GAS

TREES AIR WATER

OIL WIND SUN

WHAT CAN I DO TO HELP?

Natural resources don't go on forever. We can use them up. This is why it is important for every person to take care of the natural resources that we use for survival and for fun. You already know that it is a good idea to recycle items that can be used again, instead of just throwing them away.

Example: Oil comes from the ground. It is made when old plants and animals—fossils—decompose. After thousands of years they turn into oil and coal. Oil is used to produce many items, one of which is gasoline to power our cars. (This is why gasoline is called a fossil fuel!) What can you do to preserve this important natural resource? One thing you can do to save oil is to encourage the adults around you, including your parents, to ride bikes, walk, or use public transportation, instead of driving cars.

WHAT CAN ONE PERSON (YOU) DO TO SAVE THE NATURAL RESOURCES LISTED BELOW AS MUCH AS POSSIBLE?

Water ______________________________

____

Electricity ______________________________

____

Recreational resources like forests ______________________________

____

Natural gas, which is used to heat houses ______________________________

____

Recycling Resources

Getting and processing natural resources can require a lot of energy. This can create pollution. Recycling existing goods into other materials can save energy and reduce waste.

There are many ways each of us can help. Buying less, reusing what we can, composting, and recycling are some ways to save natural resources. How can you help?

I can buy less ______________________________

I can use less ______________________________

I can save energy by ______________________________

I can compost ______________________________

I can recycle ______________________________

I can also ______________________________

NATURAL RESOURCES WORD FIND

Natural resources are non-living things from nature that are used to support life on Earth. Can you find 6 examples of natural resources in the word find below?

P	S	N	A	O	U	W	A	T	E	R
L	B	U	S	P	Z	M	A	L	T	W
A	P	U	N	I	X	G	W	H	Z	F
N	I	B	P	L	P	Q	S	O	I	L
T	B	N	V	A	I	R	M	Z	J	F
S	N	S	V	I	O	G	P	I	F	Z
F	F	X	N	N	J	Z	H	I	N	E
V	B	Z	U	P	U	C	K	T	Q	X
F	O	S	S	I	L	F	U	E	L	S
E	P	D	U	P	D	Y	O	H	G	H

WATER AIR SOIL
PLANTS FOSSIL FUELS SUNLIGHT

THE GREAT PACIFIC GARBAGE PATCH

Things made out of plastic make our lives much easier and enjoyable. We make toys, dishes, TV cases, and storage containers out of plastic. Even cars have a lot of plastic parts. We make so many plastic water bottles that we don't know what to do with them all. Unfortunately, many of these plastic items end up in the ocean when we discard them in the wrong way.

Many of these plastic items can be found in what is called the Great Pacific Garbage Patch. This is an area in the Pacific Ocean that is about the size of the state of Texas. In this area many plastic items and small pieces of plastic items are floating around right now! Ten million tons of plastic ends up in the world's oceans and seas every year.

IN THE AREA BELOW, DRAW A PICTURE OF AT LEAST 10 PLASTIC ITEMS THAT YOU THINK MIGHT BE FLOATING AROUND IN THE GREAT PACIFIC GARBAGE PATCH. WHEN YOU ARE FINISHED, YOU WILL HAVE A PICTURE OF WHAT THE GARBAGE PATCH ACTUALLY LOOKS LIKE!

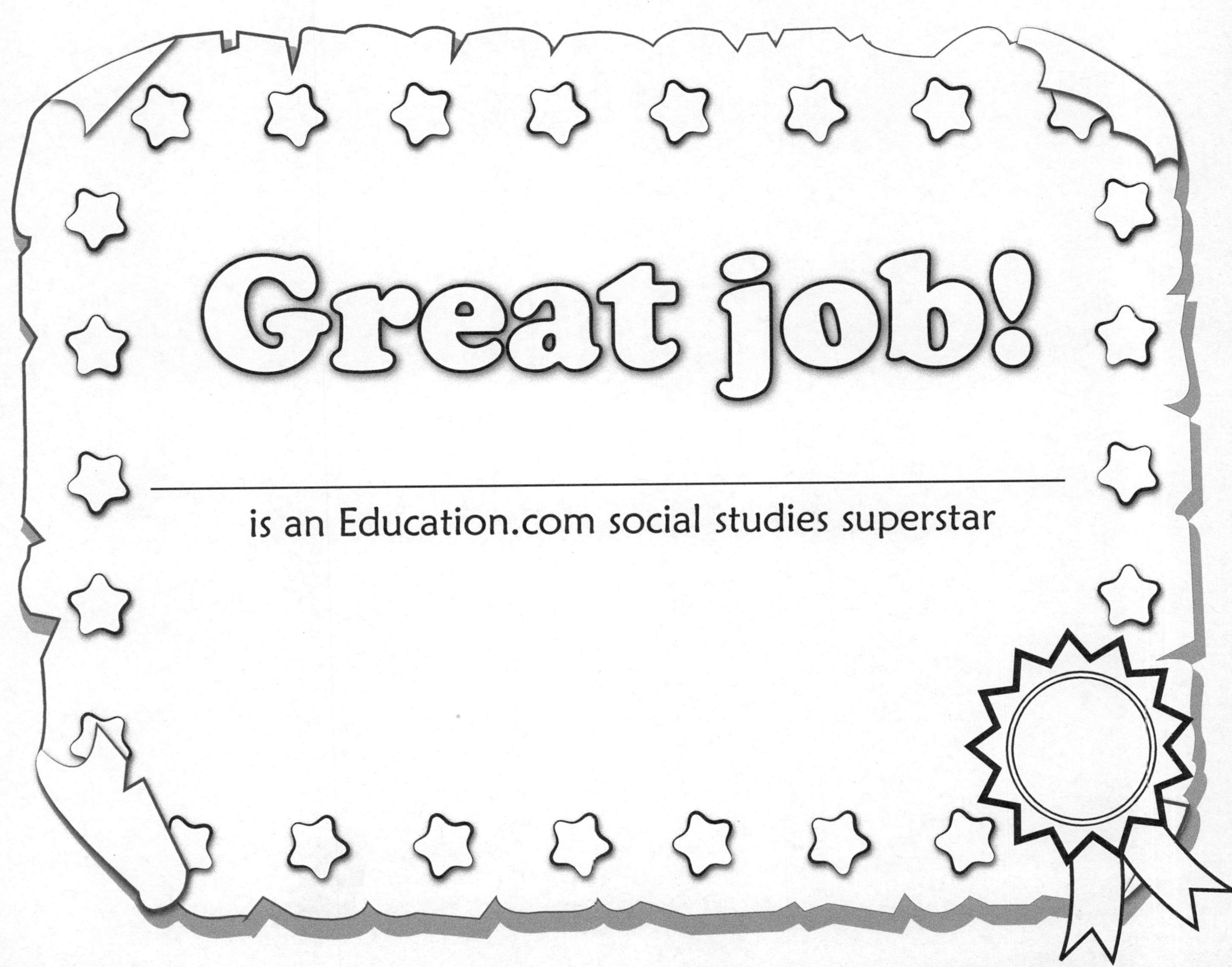
Great job!
is an Education.com social studies superstar

Can You Dig It? Rocks and Soil

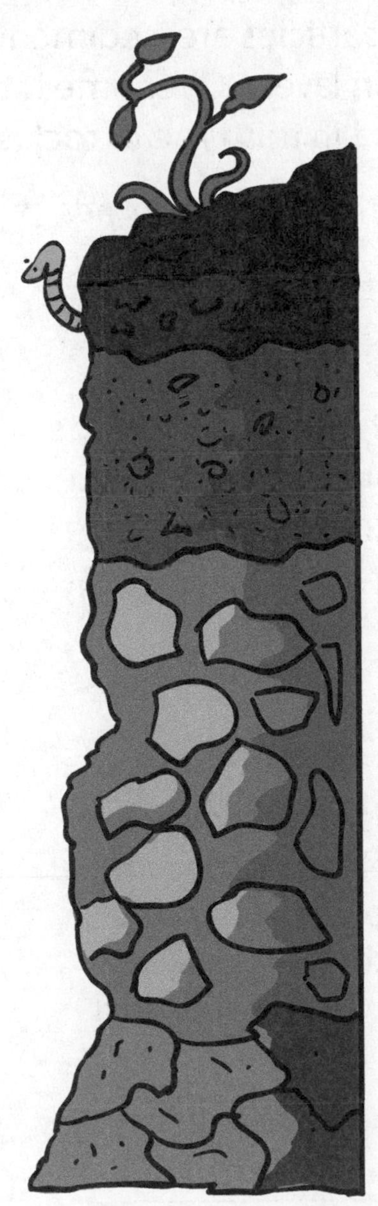

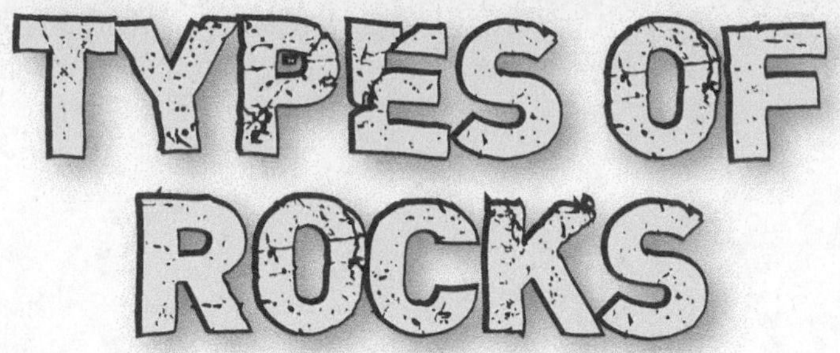

Did you know there are different types of rocks?

Sedimentary Rock

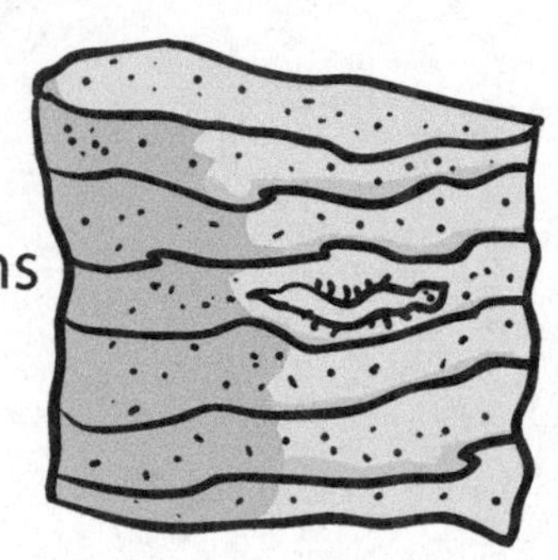

This type of rock is made out of sand, shells, pebbles and other materials. Together, these particles are "sediment". Slowly the sediment gathers up in layers. Over time it turns into rock! Fossils are usually found in this type of rock.

Can you think of a place where this type of rock can be found?

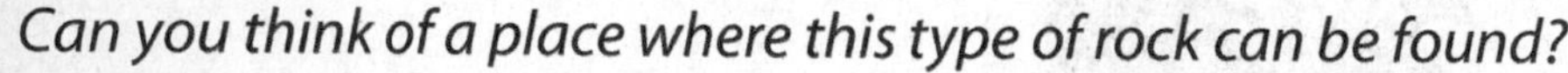

Metamorphic Rock

This type of rock is made beneath the surface of the earth. It has ribbon-like layers, caused by the heat. Some of these rocks have shiny crystals on them.

Can you think of a place where this type of rock can be found?

____

Igneous Rock

This type of rock is made from the lava of a volcano. Deep inside the earth, rocks are melted and become magma. When magma comes out of the volcano, it is called lava. If the lava cools quickly, it will make a smooth and shiny rock. If the lava cools slowly, it will form a rock with tiny holes and gas bubbles in it.

Can you think of a place where this type of rock can be found?

____

MATCH THE ROCKS

Can you identify the 3 main types of rocks?
Sedimentary, Metamorphic, and Igneous

Draw a line to connect the attribute to the correct rock type.

These rocks have small, shiny, or sparkly crystals.

These rocks have fossils or imprints of leaves, shells, or insects.

Some of these rocks may have holes like swiss cheese.

Some of these rocks are not rough but smooth and shiny like glass.

These rocks have ribbon like layers.

In these rocks you may see individual stones, pebbles, or sand grains.

WEATHERING & EROSION

Weathering and erosion work together to change the environment. In nature, large things get broken down into smaller things over time. Boulders become sand and mountains become hills.

Weathering

Weathering is what breaks down rocks and boulders and turns them into tiny pieces called sediment. There is no movement in weathering. Weathering can happen for three different reasons: plants and animals, strong weather, or chemical changes in the earth or air.

Erosion

Erosion is what moves the soil and tiny rocks that weathering leaves behind. Erosion can happen because of gravity pulling soil downhill, or because of strong weather like rain or wind.

What is happening in this picture? Which part of the scene is "weathering" and which part is "erosion?" What caused the weathering and erosion in this picture?

WEATHERING & EROSION

Weathering is what breaks down rocks and boulders and turns them into tiny pieces called *sediment*. There are three main types of weathering.

Types of Weathering

Physical Weathering / Mechanical Weathering is when nature plays a part in breaking down big rocks or mountains. There are no chemical changes in this type of weathering. Can you think of 3 types of weather that could break down rocks and soil into smaller parts?

____

Chemical Weathering is when chemical reactions break down big rocks or mountains. Can you think of one example of chemical weathering which happens when gases like nitrogen or sulfur are in the air?

____

Biological Weathering / Organic Weathering is when living things break down big rocks or mountains. This type of weathering is usually a combination of chemical and physical weathering. Can you think of 3 living things that could break down rocks and soil into smaller parts?

____

WEATHERING & EROSION

Take a look at the pictures below. Can you tell which type of weathering caused each of these things? Use your knowledge of the different types of weathering to help you make an educated guess. Write your answer under each picture.

Mechanical/Physical

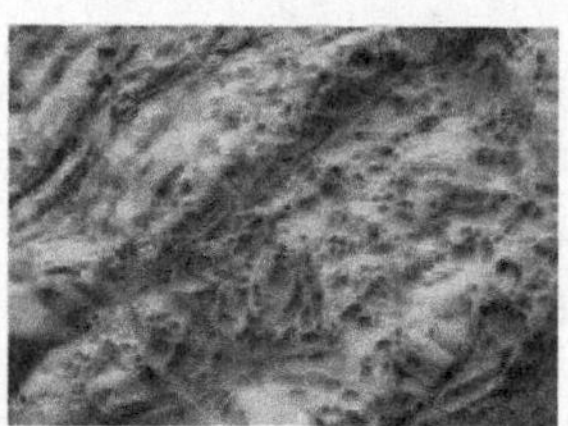

Chemical

Biological

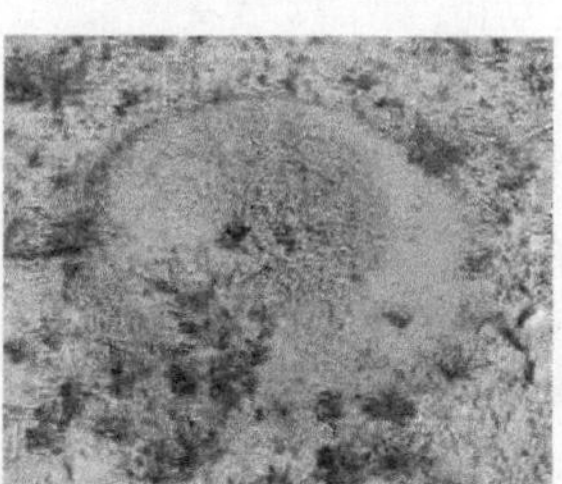

Word Bank

salt crystals	*ants*	*wind*
oxidation (rust)	*water dissolving minerals*	*bees*

Soil

Let's study the earth by learning about the part of it that we are most familiar with: the ***soil***. Soil is found on the upper-most layer of the earth's crust.

What is soil?

Soil is a mixture of four main ingredients: weathered rock, organic matter, air, and water. The weathered rock can be in the form of sand, silt, clay, pebbles, or larger rocks. Organic matter can be anything from old leaves, dead animals and plants, to microorganisms—tiny living things, like bacteria. The last two ingredients are air and water. Without air and water, the microorganisms found in soil cannot live, grow, or help dead matter to decay.

Why is soil so important?

Soil is important because it provides a place where organisms and bacteria can live. Plants rely on soil for nutrients, water, and mineral salts. Plants in turn provide the oxygen we breathe, the food we eat, the clothes we wear, and the foundation and building materials we use to make our homes. We could not meet our basic needs without soil!

Comprehension: What is the main idea of these two passages?

____

____

____

Soil

Let's study the earth by learning about the part of it that we are most familiar with: the ***soil***. Soil is found on the upper-most layer of the earth's crust.

How is soil formed?

Soil is formed in several ways. The break down, or ***weathering***, of rocks is one way soil is formed. Water, wind, and ice also help to create soil. Earth materials are carried by water, wind, and ice, and are eventually dropped in places where they settle and mix with other materials to become soil. But the key ingredient to the making of soil is the living and once-living things that are found in it. These living and dead organisms are called ***organic matter***. They turn the sand, silt, and rock pieces into a mixture that is perfect for helping plants and animals to live and grow.

Did you know…
Tiny plants can break down big rocks!

Comprehension: List 5 things that can break down rock into soil.

Types of Soil

Soil differs greatly from place to place, but all soil is made up of different amounts of three types of particles: sand, silt, and clay.

What are the types of soil particles?

Sand is the largest particle found in soil. When you rub it, it feels rough and gritty. Sand does not have many nutrients, but it dries quickly after rainfall, and it is good for *drainage*, which means it lets water flow through it easily.

Silt is the medium-sized particle found in soil. Silt feels smooth and powdery when dry, and it feels slippery when wet. Silt can be packed down into a crust that makes it harder for water and air to pass through it.

Clay is the smallest particle found in soil. Clay feels smooth and hard as stone when dry, and it feels sticky when wet. While clay can hold many nutrients, it does not allow much air or water to pass through. Too much clay can make the soil heavy and not good for growing plants.

Loam is a mix of sand, silt and clay. It is the best type of soil for growing plants. Loam breaks up easily and holds moisture and nutrients, while still allowing some water and air to pass through.

Types of Soil

Response Questions

Which soil type can become hard as stone when dry? ____________________

Which soil type dries out quickly after a rainfall? ________________________

Which soil type would be best for building a structure? __________________

Which soil type would a gardener need to break up every now and then to allow more drainage? _________________

Which soil type would a cactus do well in? _________________

TRY THIS!

Dig down at least six inches and grab a handful of soil. Soak it with water and roll it into a ball in your hand.

Sand

If you cannot make a ball out of it, it is mostly ***sand***.

Silt

If it forms a loose ball but crumbles when squeezed it is mostly ***silt***.

Clay

If it forms a packed ball and can be reshaped into a snake, it is mostly ***clay***.

Types of Soil Textures

Soil differs greatly from place to place, but all soil is composed of varying amounts of clay, silt, and sand. You can determine the components of soil by feeling its texture, which is based on the size of its particles.

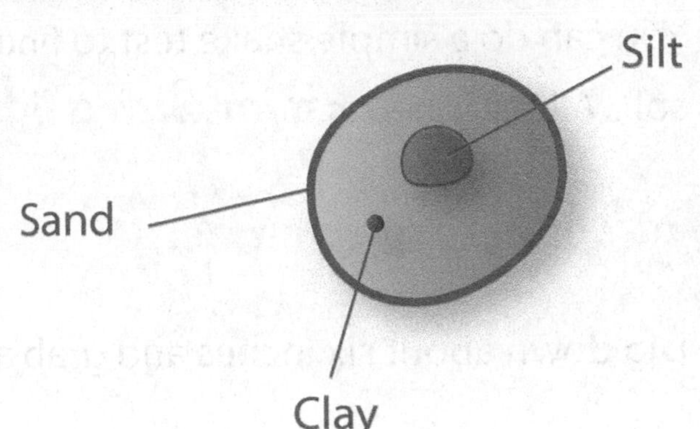

Soil Characteristics

Finish this chart by filling in the textures and sizes for each type of soil particle.

	Clay	Silt	Sand
Texture			
Particle Size			
Advantage	*holds onto water and nutrients*	*allows some drainage and holds nutrients*	*good drainage, air passes through it easily*
Disadvantage	*gets heavy with water, hardens when dry*	*easily packed down, causing less water and air to pass through*	*does not hold nutrients*

Soil Shake Up

You can do a simple shake test to find out how much clay, silt, and sand is in your soil. All you need is ***a jar with a lid***, a handful of ***soil***, and ***water***.

Soil shake-up activity!

Dig down about six inches and grab a handful of soil.

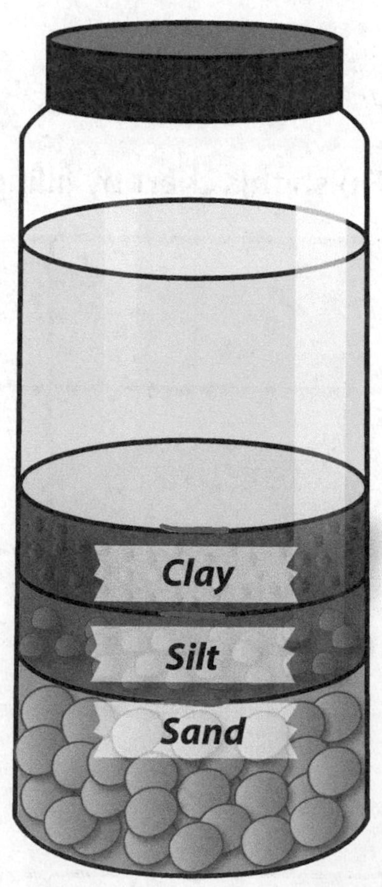

Put the soil into a jar. Fill it to the top with water and close the lid tightly. Shake the jar for a few minutes.

Set the jar down. Look for large particles of sand, which should settle at the bottom of the jar. Mark the top of this layer with a pen or tape.

Wait an hour. Look for a layer of smaller silt particles, which should settle above the sand. Mark the top of this layer.

Wait a day and look at the jar again. The water should be clear. Look for a layer of the smallest clay particles to settle on top of the silt. Mark the top of this layer.

The size of the layers tells you how much sand, silt, or clay is in your soil.

Soil Shake Up

Here are some empty jars to draw your own soil layers.

Soil Shake Up

Look at the three sample results below. For each jar, record whether the soil contains mostly ***clay***, ***silt***, or ***sand***.

Loam

The best soil for growing is loam. It has equal parts clay, silt, and sand. Draw what the results of the shake test will look like if your soil is loamy.

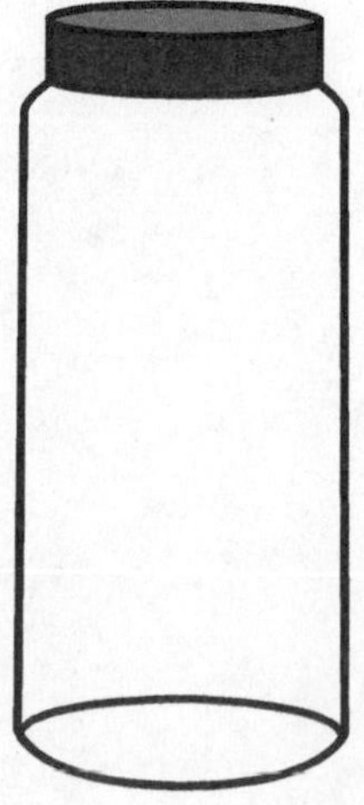

Soil Layers

Soil is made up of distinct horizontal layers. If you could take an elevator ride through the earth's surface you would pass several distinct layers.

What are the layers of soil?

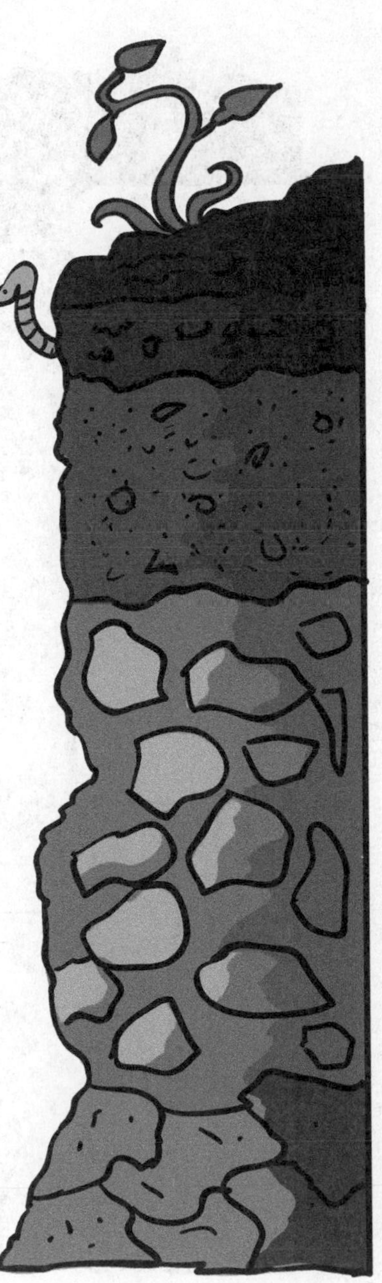

The ***humus*** is the topmost layer of soil. It contains quite a bit of living material, plants, decaying leaves, needles, moss, and more. This layer is thin and very dark in color.

The ***topsoil*** is the next layer down. It is made mostly of minerals, and most plant roots live here. This layer is also dark in color due to the amount of decaying plant and animal matter.

The ***subsoil layer*** is next. It is made of sand, silt, and clay that have not been broken down all the way, so it usually has less organic material in it. It is also lighter in color.

The ***parent material*** is the next layer down. It is mostly rock that has been slightly weathered. Not many things live down here, except for the biggest tree roots.

The ***bedrock*** is the lowest layer of soil. It is a solid rock layer.

Soil

Let's play a game! Help Mr. Worm back up to the top, starting at the red dot. Can you name all the layers in soil? Write the names in the blank labels.

Soil

Let's play a game! Can you find all the words about soil? Circle them as you find them. Have fun!

B	S	D	W	H	U	M	U	S	H
E	I	N	E	D	C	S	C	O	S
D	L	U	A	E	O	O	E	R	A
R	T	T	T	C	M	I	R	G	N
O	C	R	H	O	P	L	O	A	D
C	L	I	E	M	O	L	S	N	L
K	A	E	R	P	S	I	I	I	O
E	Y	N	I	O	T	I	O	C	A
X	F	T	N	S	H	D	N	Q	M
W	I	S	G	E	N	T	S	R	A

Word Bank

Sand Silt Clay Loam Soil Compost Nutrients Organic Decompose Humus Bedrock Weathering Erosion

Compost

What is compost?

Compost is ***organic*** material that has been ***decomposed***. Organic material is anything from the earth — fruits, veggies, plants, dirt, and more When organic material decomposes, it breaks down into nutrients that fertilize the soil. Some people make their own compost to help their gardens or farm crops grow, but nature also makes its own compost! When plants die or when leaves fall from trees, they form ***mulch*** that protects the soil. Over time the dead leaves decompose into nutrients that feed the new plants. This is nature's way of recycling old materials.

DRAW THE CYCLE — The compost cycle is a type of life cycle, similar to the water cycle. Fill in the pictures to show each step of the compost cycle.

Organic — natural, living matter

Decomposed — when something is broken down into smaller parts

Mulch — a material, such as dead leaves or bark, spread around or over a plant to enrich or protect the soil

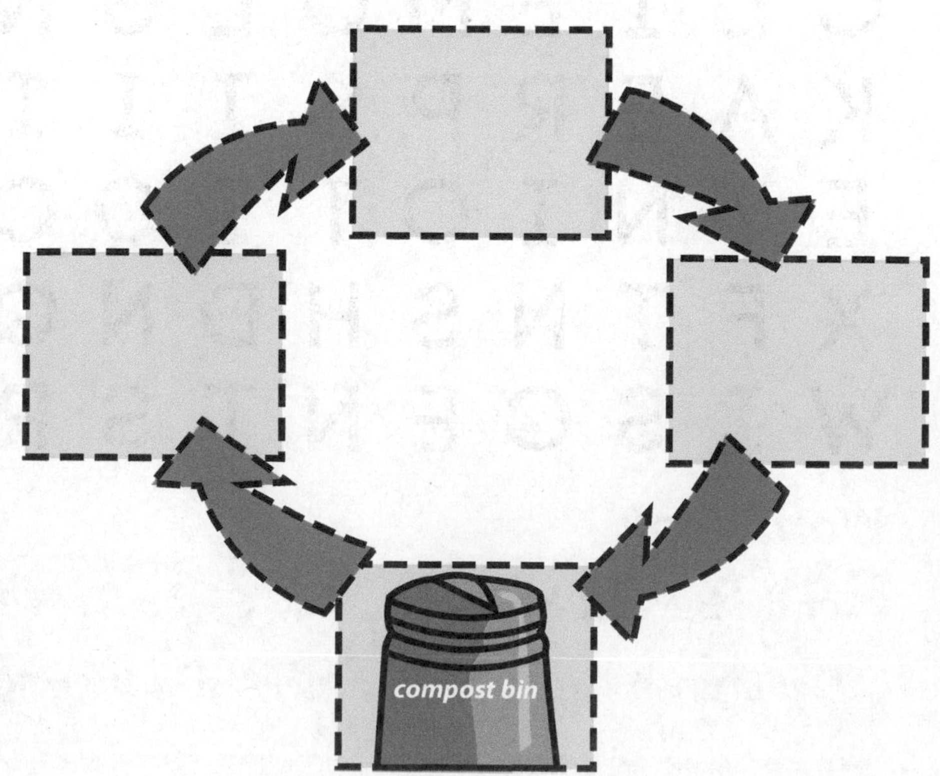

Compost

Compost is *organic material*—such as leaves, fruits and veggies—that has been *decomposed*, or broken down into smaller parts. Compost helps give nutrients to the soil, and helps make new plants grow. You can recycle leaves and other plant materials at home by setting up a compost bin!

Recipe for Compost

-Brown stuff
-Green stuff
-Air
-Water

The microorganisms (tiny living things, like bacteria or fungus) that recycle leaves and other plant parts need an even mix of brown stuff and green stuff to munch on.

Brown stuff is dead, dried plant parts like leaves and pine needles. Brown stuff is high in the element carbon, which will help provide energy to this mix.

Green stuff is fresh, living parts like grass clippings, kitchen vegetable scraps, weeds and other plants. Green stuff is high in the element nitrogen, which helps produce more protein.

Air and water are two key ingredients to help the microorganisms in the compost to live and work. The material in your compost bin cannot work if it is sealed off from any air or water source.

Compost

Good Compost Conditions

Selecting a spot

Find a nice spot in the yard to start your compost pile. It should be out of the way but easy to reach with plenty of room to work around. Some good places would be near your garden or in a back corner of the yard. It is also a good idea to choose a location close to a source of water.

TIP: Some people like to keep a mini compost bin in their kitchen to collect scraps of fruit and veggie peels, eggshells, coffee grounds, and other kitchen waste This is a great way to recycle kitchen trash that you normally throw away!

Building your compost pile

It's easiest to build a compost pile in layers of ingredients. Start with the brown stuff by spreading a layer of old leaves or pine needles about 6 inches thick. Next, add the green stuff, including grass clippings and scraps from your mini kitchen waste bin. Finally, sprinkle a shovelful of soil to add microorganisms into the pile.

Speeding up the process

The microorganisms in the compost take a long time to break down the organic material. If you want faster compost, you can mix the ingredients every few weeks. This is not necessary, but it can help the process.

Your Compost Pile

How big is your pile?______________________________

What does it smell like?______________________________

What kinds of things are in your compost?

____

Compost

What is compost?

What are the 4 main ingredients in the recipe for compost?

Can you think of any items that ***should not*** *be put in your compost?*

What is "brown stuff" and what is "green stuff"?

Compost

DOs and DON'Ts of Compost

What goes in your compost bin? Cut and paste the materials on the next page,and put them in the appropriate spots on this chart! Can you think of any more materials to add to the chart?

DO put in your compost	*DON'T put in your compost*

Compost

Cut out these items and place them in the correct spots on the chart.

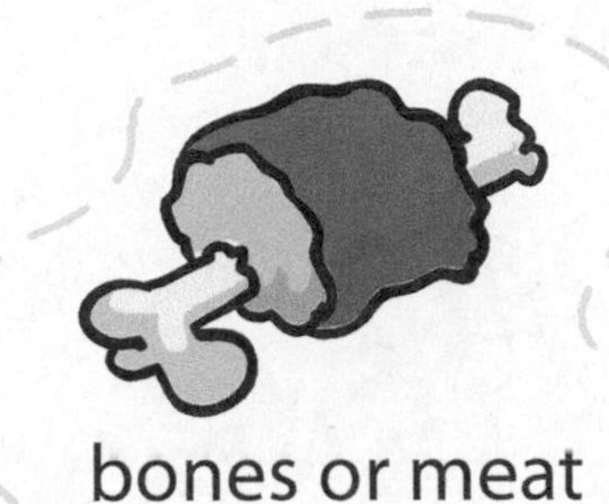

bones or meat

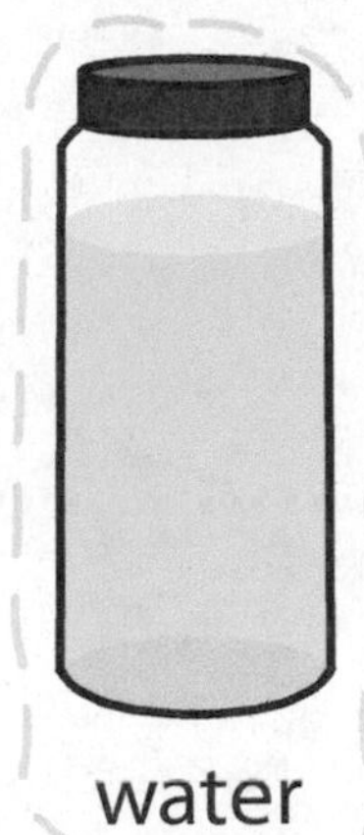

water

newspaper

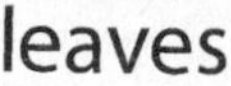

leaves

fruit and vegetable scraps

dairy products:
milk, cheese, or ice cream

oily foods

sawdust

grass clippings

Great job!
is an Education.com science superstar

Tree-mendous

Parts of a Tree

Trees have different parts that serve their own special functions. The **primary root** of the tree is the thickest. It holds the plant in the soil and takes in water and nutrients. The **secondary root** branches from the primary root. It helps support the tree, and also takes in water and nutrients from the soil. A tree's **leaves** use light and energy from the sun to make sugar and carbon dioxide to feed the plant. Lastly, the stem or **trunk** keeps distance between the leaves and and the soil while carrying nutrients from the roots to the upper parts of the tree.

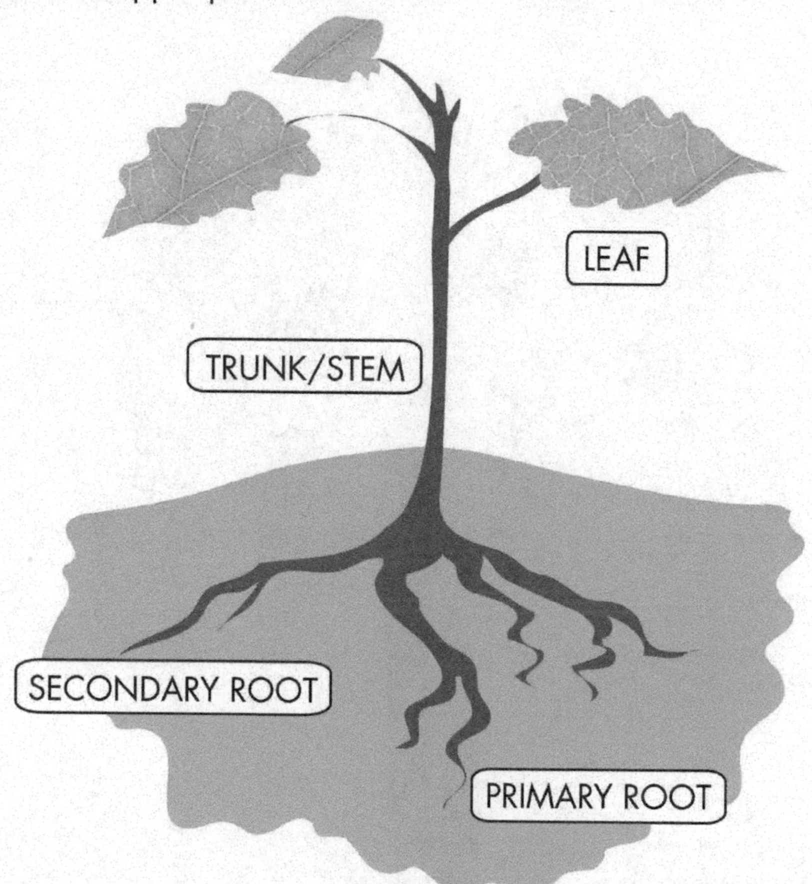

I take in lots of water from the soil and hold the tree firmly in place. I am the...

________________ .

I keep distance between the leaves and the soil, while delivering food. I am the...

________________ .

I use light and heat to make food for the rest of the tree. I am the...

________________ .

I assist the larger root in supporting the tree, as well as taking in water. I am the...

________________ .

HOW TO DRAW A TREE

Follow these easy steps to turn a couple of lines into a lush apple tree.

Start by drawing the trunk.

Next, add some branches.

Then, add the leaves.

Finish off by adding some fruit.

Don't forget to add color to your final picture!

TREE SCRAMBLE

Unscramble the letters to reveal parts of a tree. You can experiment with different words from the box below.

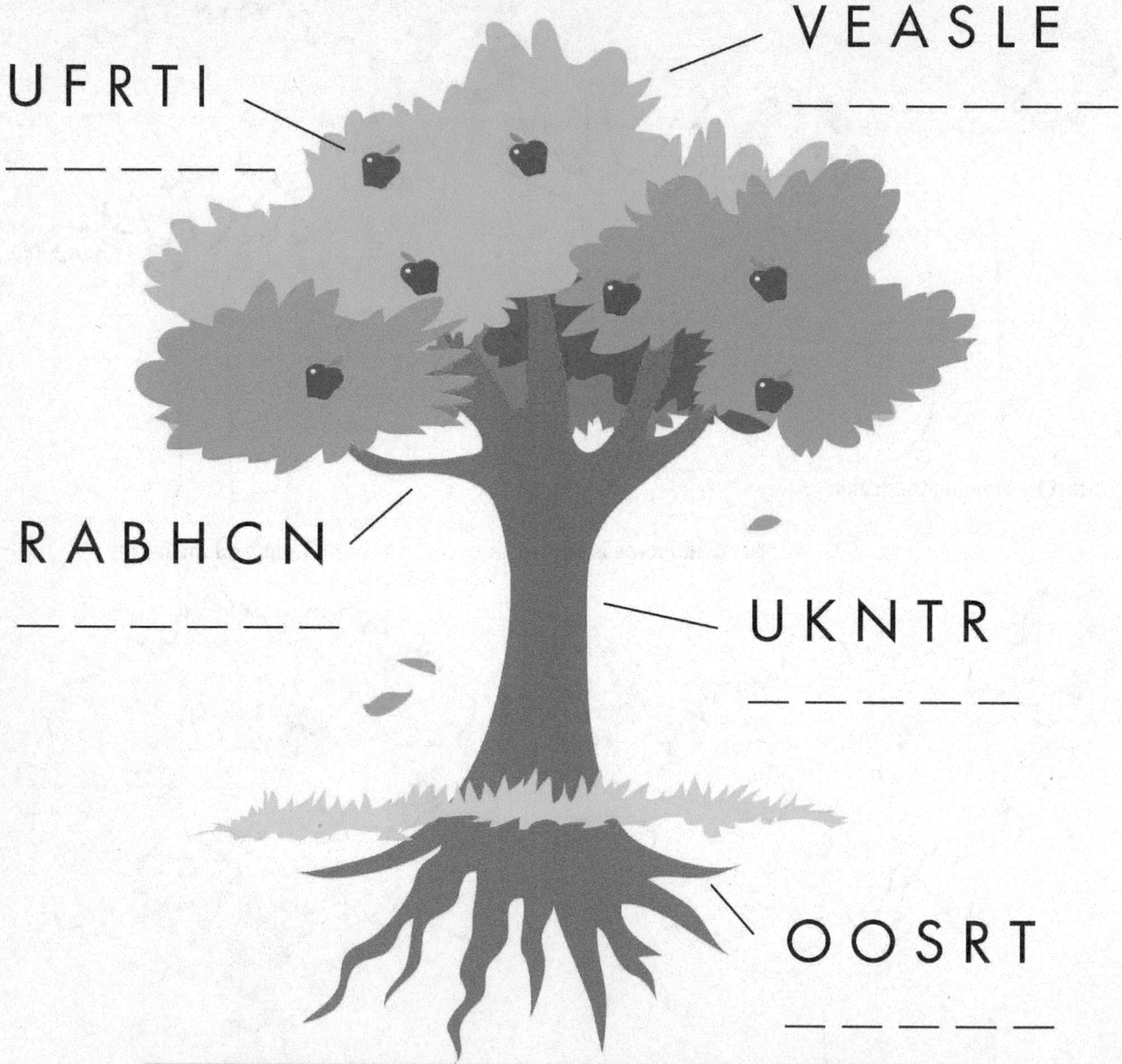

UFRTI

_ _ _ _ _

VEASLE

_ _ _ _ _ _

RABHCN

_ _ _ _ _ _

UKNTR

_ _ _ _ _

OOSRT

_ _ _ _ _

BRANCH	LEAVES	STUMP	GRASS
FRUIT	NEEDLES	TALL	NEST
THORN	ROOTS	GREEN	TRUNK

TREE MEASURING

Use a ruler to measure this tree. First, write down your estimate of the length to the nearest inch and centimeter. Then, use a ruler to perform a more accurate measurement, again rounding to the nearest inch or centimeter.

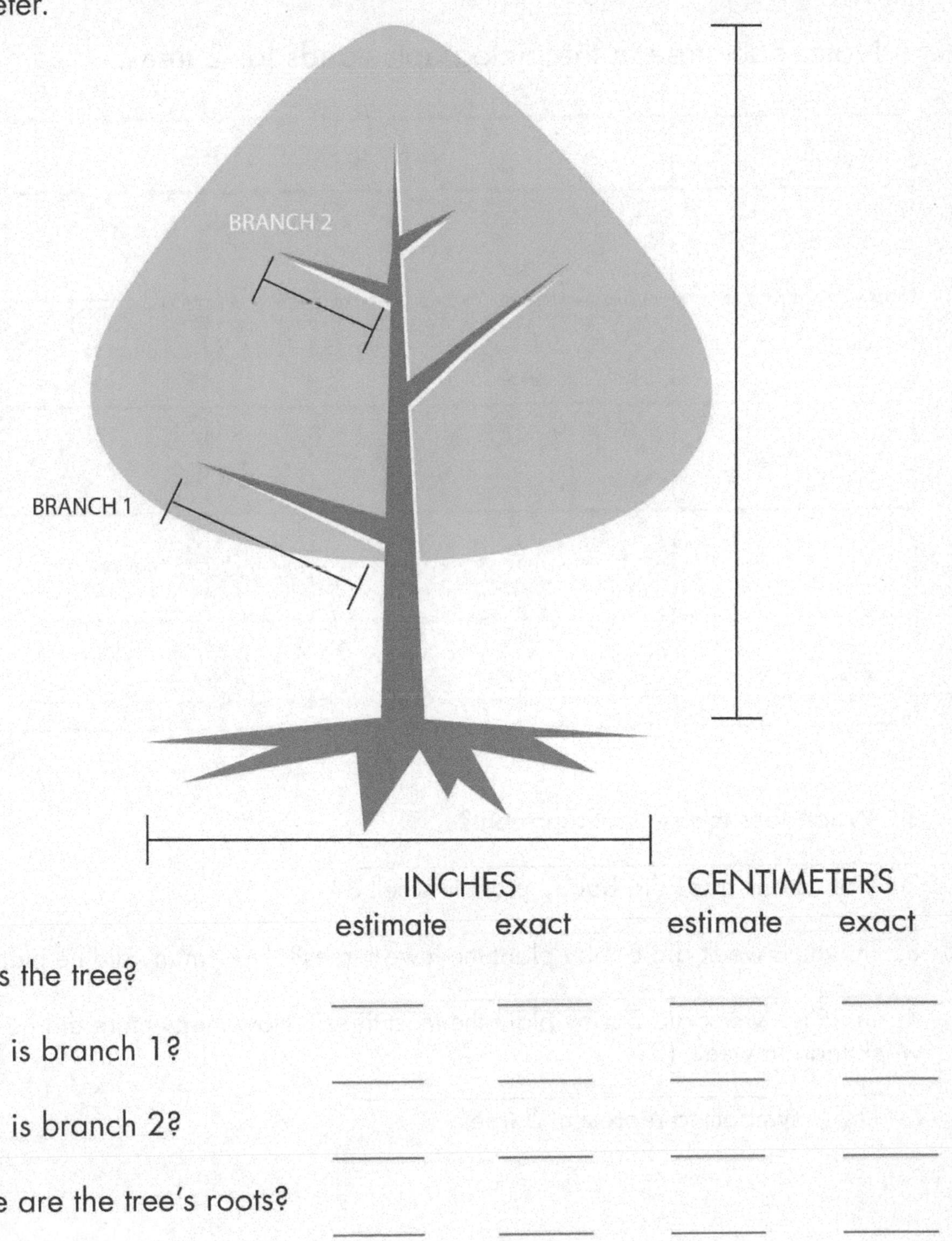

	INCHES		CENTIMETERS	
	estimate	exact	estimate	exact
How tall is the tree?	_____	_____	_____	_____
How long is branch 1?	_____	_____	_____	_____
How long is branch 2?	_____	_____	_____	_____
How wide are the tree's roots?	_____	_____	_____	_____

GROWING TREES

Trees are important natural resources. Find out how many trees Bobby planted in the past few weeks by reading the pictograph below. Then, answer the questions.

Note: each tree in the pictograph stands for 2 trees.

WEEK	NUMBER OF TREES
WEEK 1	
WEEK 2	
WEEK 3	
WEEK 4	
WEEK 5	

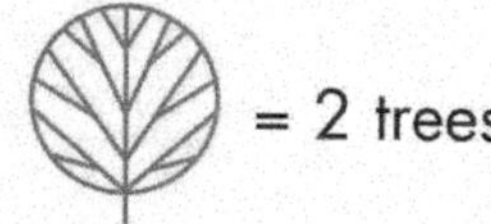
= 2 trees

1. What does this symbol represent?

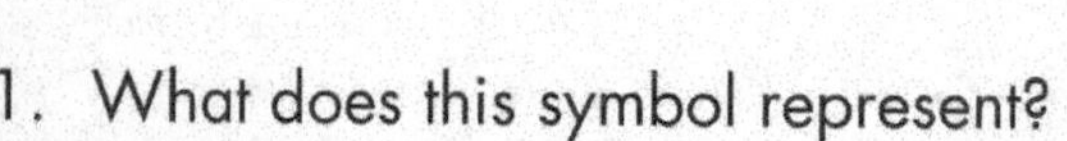

2. How many trees did Bobby plant in week 3?

3. In which week did Bobby plant the fewest trees? How many did he plant that week?

4. In which week did Bobby plant the most trees? How many more did he plant in that week than in week 1?

5. Draw symbols to represent 5 trees.

A TREE FOR ALL SEASONS

Some trees keep green leaves or needles all year long. These types of trees are called evergreens. Other trees have leaves that change, depending on the amount of sunlight they receive and the temperature that surrounds them. Trees that lose their leaves will shed them during the cold and dark winter months. During the spring, new leaves grow, and they are green in the warmer climate. They continue to sway in the breeze during the warm and sunny summer months. When fall arrives and the sun is not shining quite as bright, the leaves will change color.

Directions: Color the pictures below. Cut out the pictures and paste them into the box with the correct season.

SPRING	SUMMER
FALL	WINTER

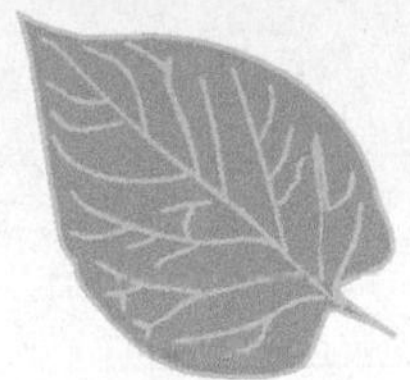

How Do Apples Grow?

Some apple trees will grow over 40 feet high and live over 100 years!

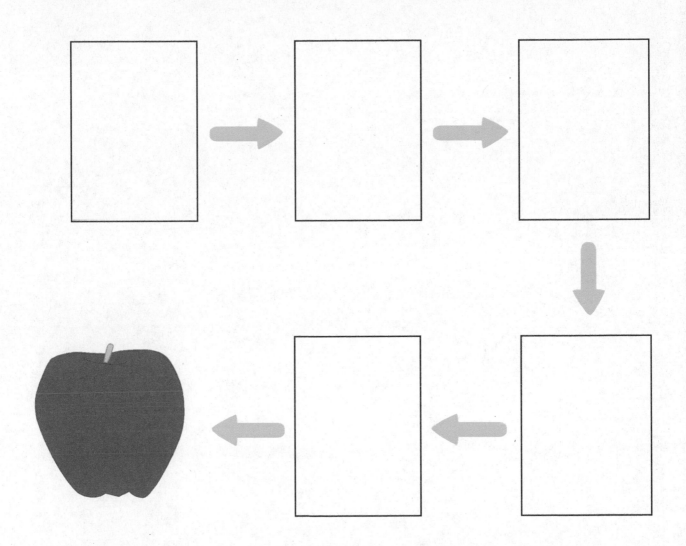

CUT OUT THE PEICES AND PASTE THEM IN ORDER OF GROWTH

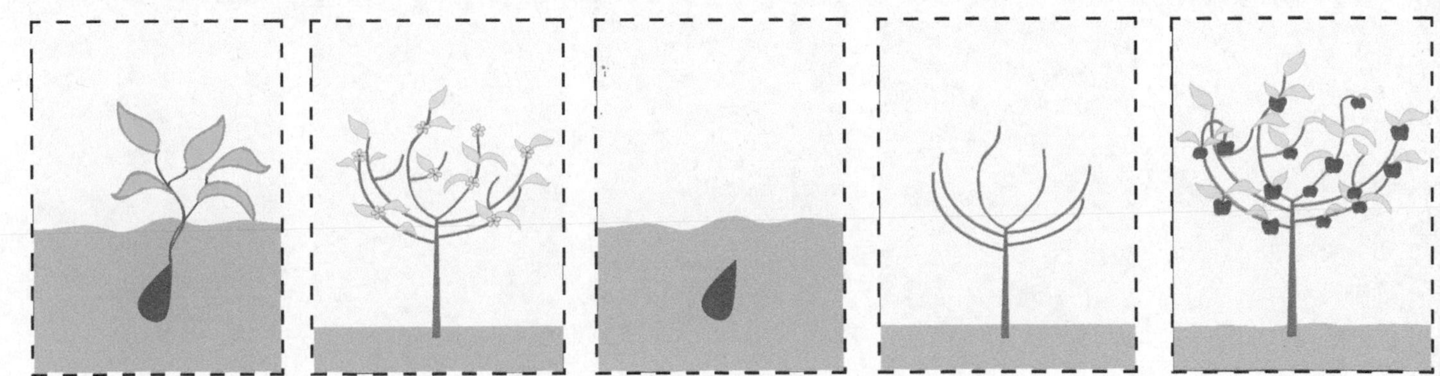

TREE TREATS

For every tree or plant below, draw a snack you can eat thanks to it in the space provided.

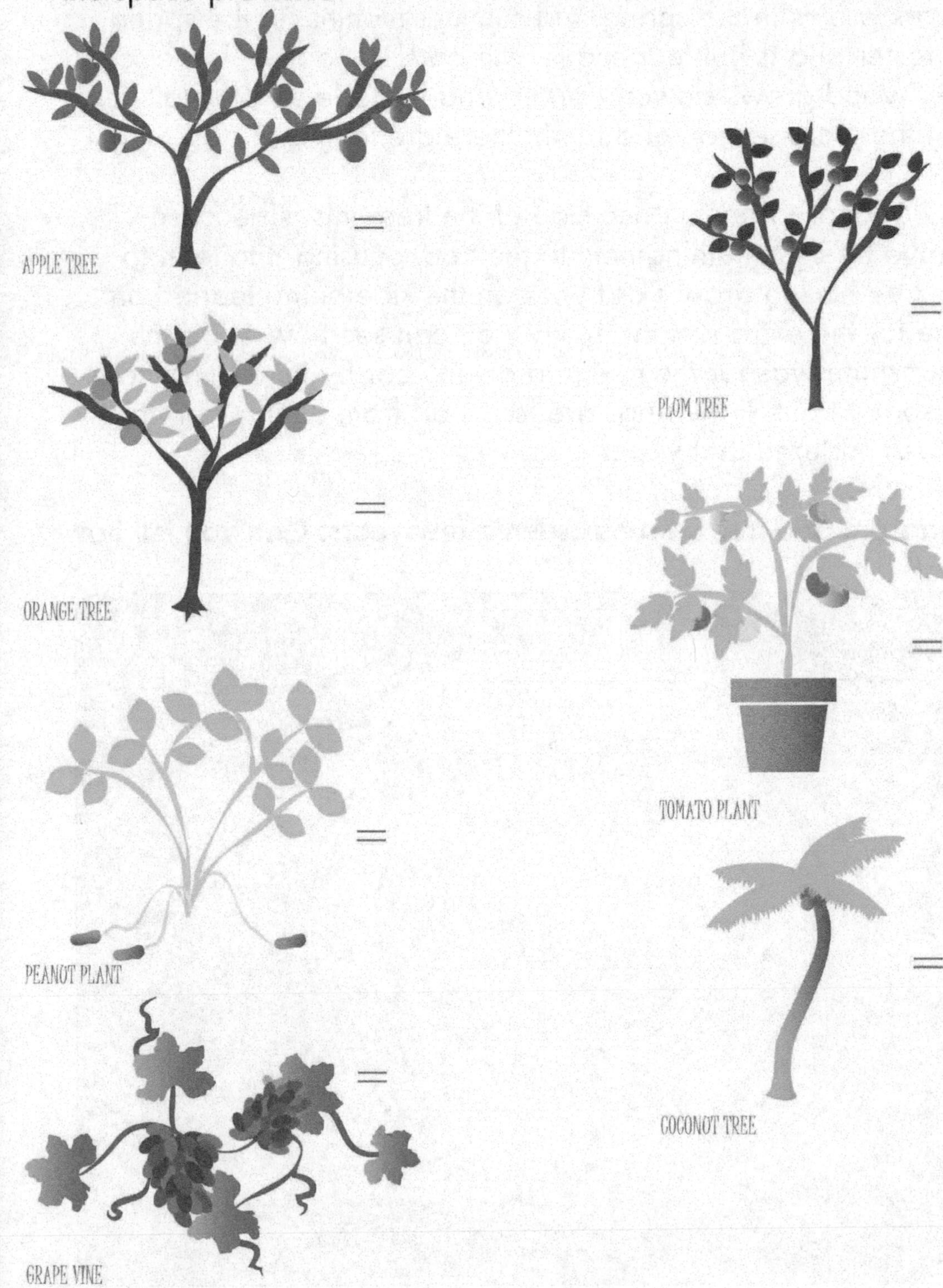

READING TREE RINGS

Every year a tree grows, new layers of bark are formed. For each year the tree has been alive, a ring can be seen in the cross-section of the trunk. New bark grows in the spring and summer months. In the spring, wood grows faster and is lighter because the bark is made of larger cells. In the summer, wood grows slower, darker, and is made up of small cells. This is seen in the cross-section of a trunk; there are light and dark rings!

The rings may appear larger on one side of the tree; this is because there might have been something next to the tree, causing it to lean to one side. The tree had to grow extra bark on the side being leaned on to compensate for the extra weight. Lastly, you can see how good the rainfall and sunshine was for the tree in a given year by inspecting how the rings are spaced out. If the rings are far apart from each other, then the tree was well-nurtured that year.

Below is a diagram of a tree who has seen a few years. Can you tell how old it is?

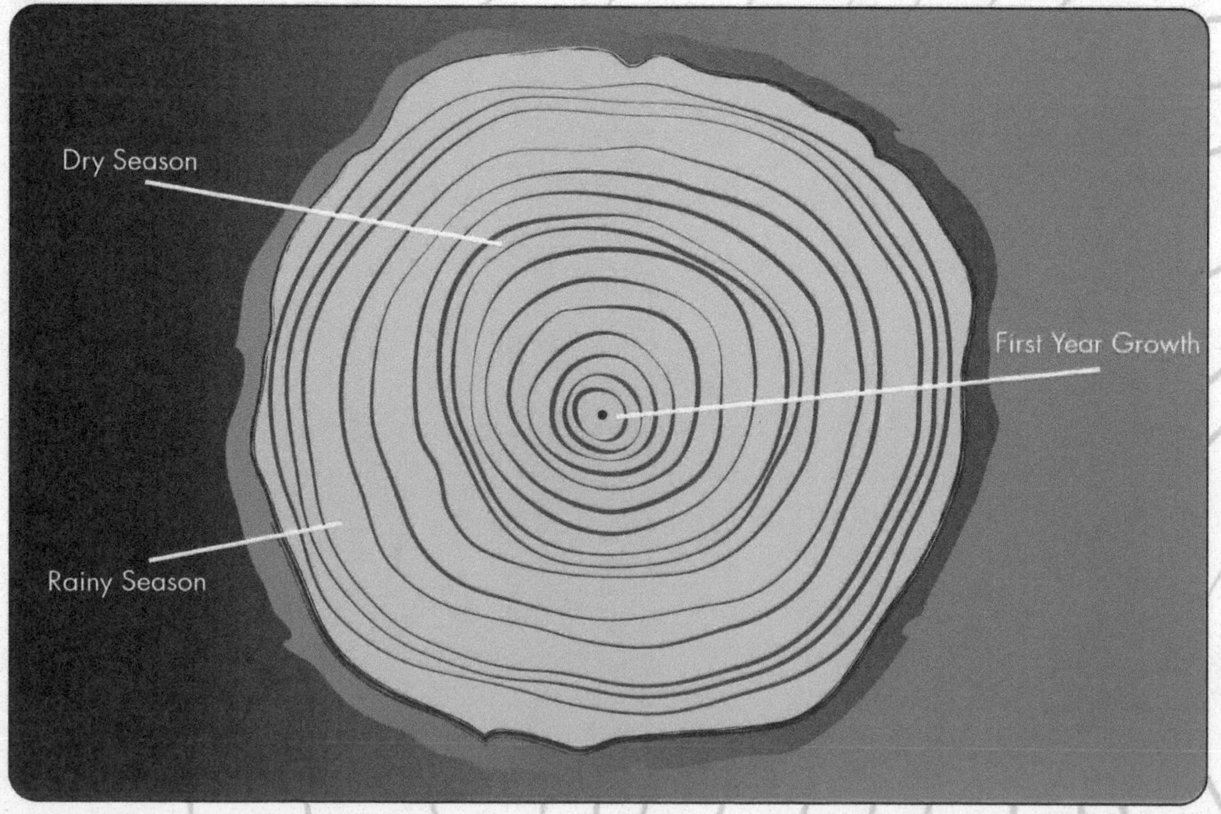

READING TREE RINGS

Use what you've learned to create a set of tree rings with a history of your own. Consider what you've learned about telling how old a tree is, what kind of weather it received, and whether or not it leaned to one side or another.

HOW OLD IS THAT TREE?

What You Need:

Tree
Measuring tape
Marker
Pen
Paper
Helper

What You Do:

Help your child find a tree that is at least as tall as a grown-up and have your child wrap the measuring tape around the widest part of the trunk. (A grown-up might need to help with this part!) The distance around the trunk of a tree is called the circumference. Write this measurement down on a piece of paper.

The measurement of the circumference in inches is also the approximate age of the tree in years!

Did You Know?

Every year a new layer of growth occurs just under the bark. Some trees like firs and redwoods may grow more than this in a year, while others like cedars may grow less. This method is a good rule of thumb to estimate the age of a tree.

TREE STUMP WORD SEARCH

Trees are separated into two categories: coniferous and deciduous. Conifer trees have long, thin needle leaves, and bear cones (pinecones!). Deciduous trees have broad leaves that change color with the seasons.

Try to find different types of coniferous and deciduous trees hidden in the word search below.

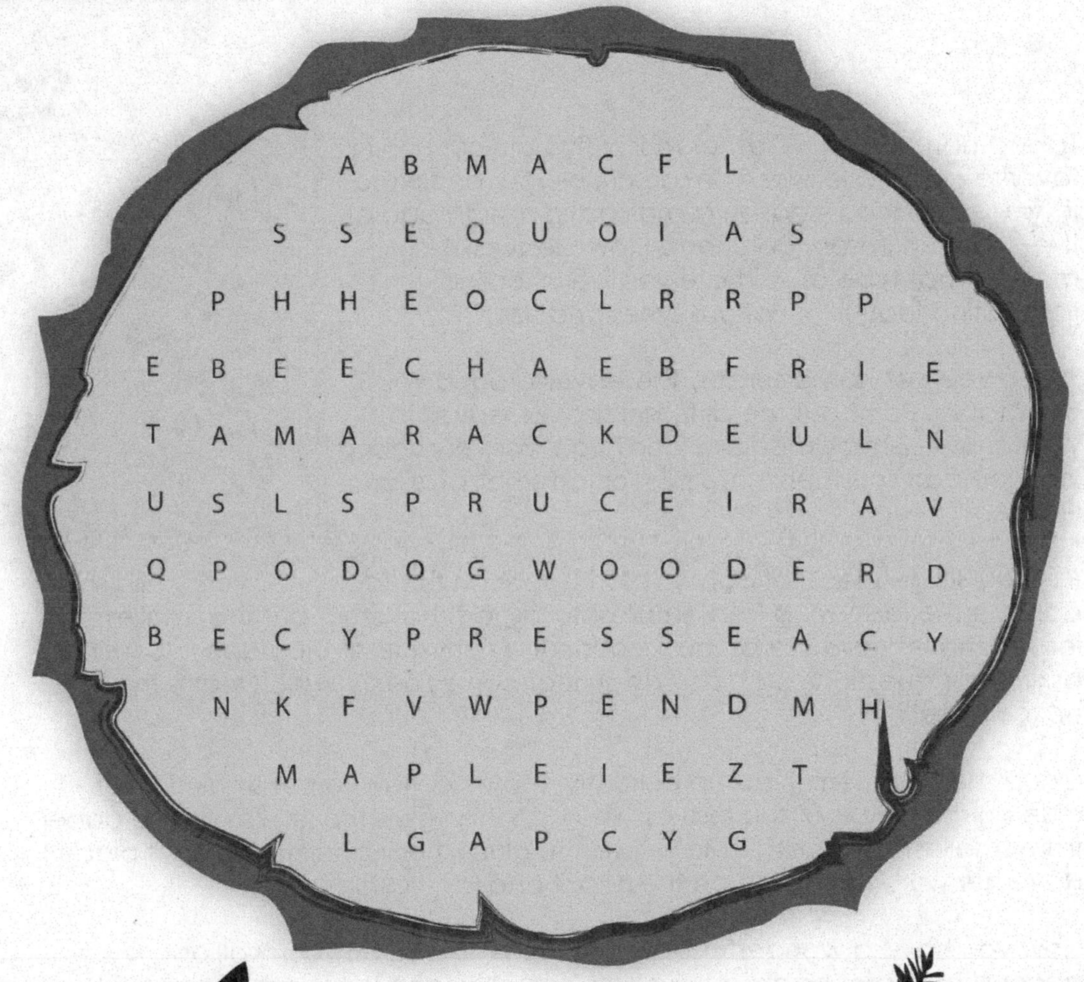

Deciduous		Coniferous	
Ash	Dogwood	Cedar	Pine
Aspen	Maple	Fir	Sequoia
Beech	Mulberry	Hemlock	Spruce
Cypress	Oak	Larch	Tamarack

SORTING AND ORDERING LEAVES

What You Need:

4 to 5 different-sized leaves
12"x18" construction paper, or, two 8.5"x11" papers taped together
Glue

What You Do:

1. Take a nature walk. Gather four or five of your child's favorite colored leaves from a park or your backyard. If you live in a four-season climate take advantage of the brilliant crimson, gold, and brown leaves. No matter what type of climate you live in, collect interesting leaves of various types and sizes.

2. When you get home spread the leaves around your work table. Point out the different sizes of leaves to your child — small, medium, and large. For very young kids you can sort them into piles of just small and large leaves.

3. Put your large piece of construction paper on the table. Tell your child she can line the leaves up from smallest to largest. Have her put the smallest leaf to the left and the biggest leaf on the right side of the paper. Continue asking her questions such as "Which leaf comes next? Which leaf is the next biggest?"

4. Once she has them lined up correctly, show her how to put small dots of glue on the backs of the leaves. She can then glue the leaves on the paper from smallest to largest. (Make sure she glues them back to the right place.) Have her write her name on the paper and lay it aside to dry.

5. Now you have a wonderful leaf collection to hang on your wall as decoration. Refer back to this helpful visual whenever you ask your child questions about relative size. You can also use it to discuss with her the four seasons and how the trees change with each season.

ACTIVITY: LEAF WALK

Go for a walk with an adult and collect 10 leaves with different shapes. Once you're back home, use this chart to figure out what type of leaves you found.

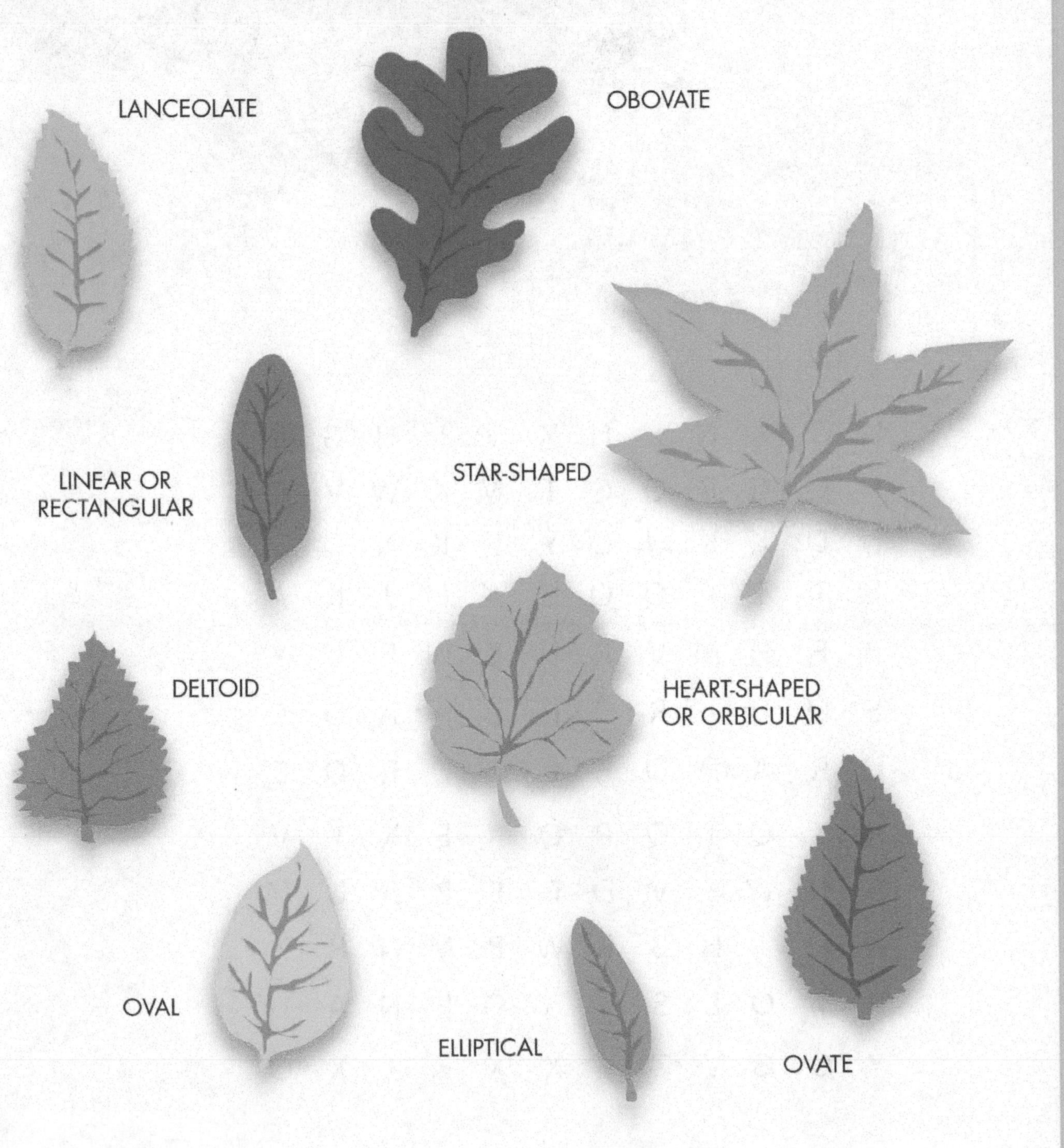

TREE CLIMBERS

The animals listed on the tree are all good climbers. Can you find them in the word search below?

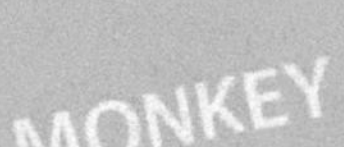

MONKEY

BEAR

RACCOON

SQUIRREL

SLOTH

KOALA

FOX

LEOPARD

W S A N I N Y V I N G K

N O O R O Q T M K W V C

N D K K N O Y E K N O M

L T T I Q Q C A F J K A

B F H M V K L C W E L Y

S Q U I R R E L A A D F

D R A P O E L B O R O E

K X Q T Q P Q K E X Y V

A N W S V D F E B A U M

X P J H B R W B M N R Z

H T O L S V A O F N A L

Y G G V Z Y X X E J X O

THE RAINFOREST IS HOME

The tropical rainforest is a place where the weather is warm all year round and a great amount of rain falls. Because of the warm climate and large amounts of rain, a tropical rainforest has more kinds of trees than any other area in the world. Over half of all types of plants and animals live in rainforests, and tropical rainforests produce almost half of the Earth's oxygen. Unfortunately, the rainforests of the world are being destroyed and damaged.

Directions: Think of 5 ways you can help save these animals and their homes. Talk to an adult about your ideas.

THE RAINFOREST IS HOME

Directions: Find and circle each hidden rainforest animal in the picture below. A few may be hidden in the background.

Harpy Eagle	Dawn Bat	African Forest Elephant	Southern Cassowary
King Cobra	Chimpanzee	Golden Lion Tamarin	
Bengal Tiger	Two-toed Sloth	Yellow-browed Toucanet	

TREES ARE HOME TO MANY DIFFERENT ANIMALS

Trees are home to many different animals if you look hard enough. Can you find all the tenants taking up residence in this tree? After you find them, start coloring!

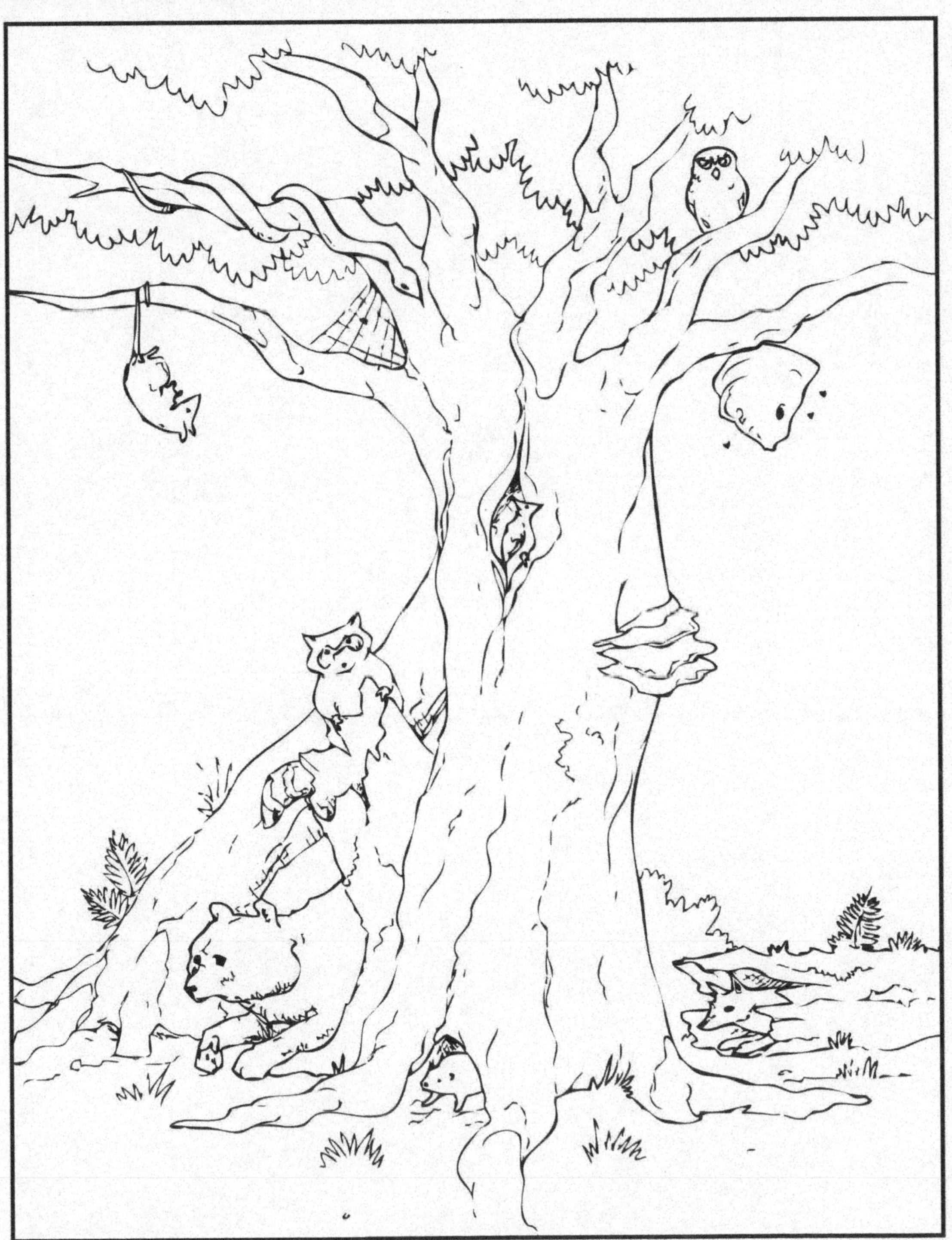

Great job!
is an Education.com science superstar

ANSWERS

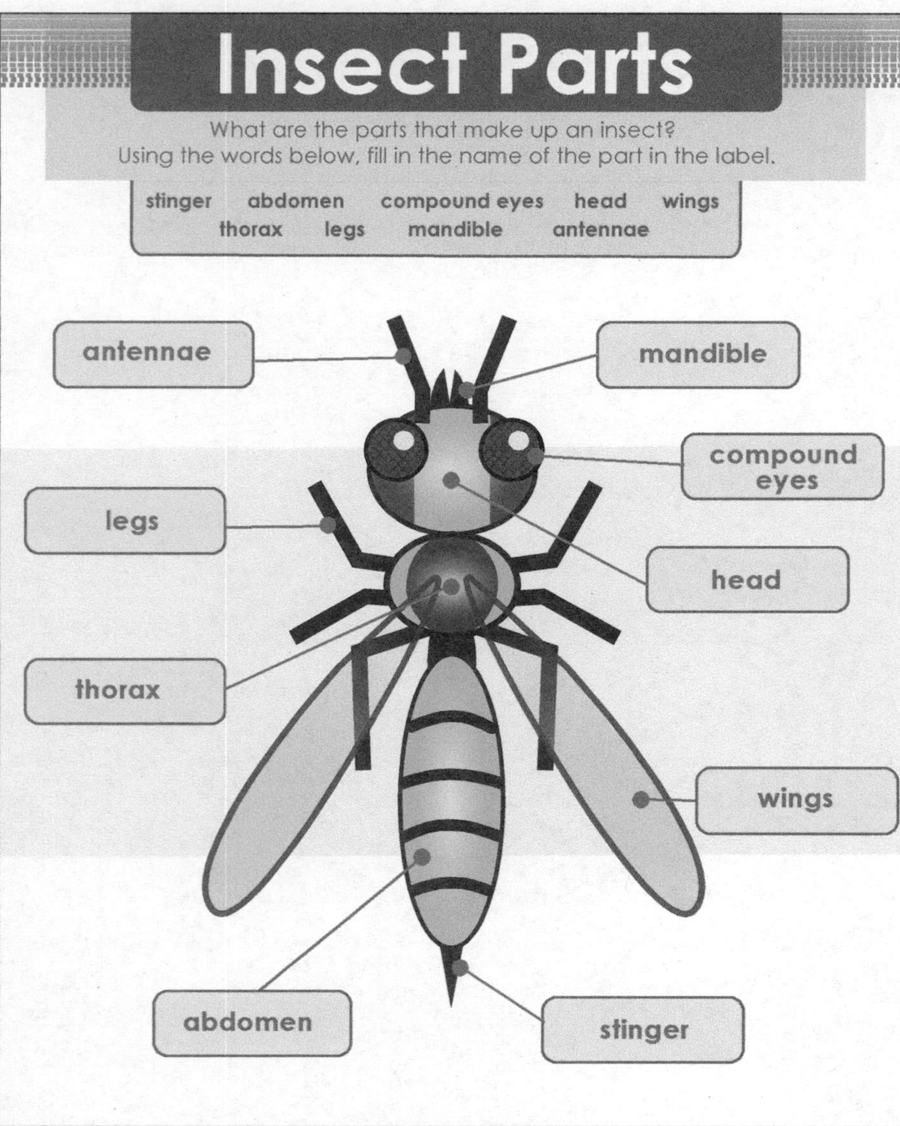
Insect Parts
What are the parts that make up an insect?
Using the words below, fill in the name of the part in the label.
stinger abdomen compound eyes head wings
thorax legs mandible antennae
antennae
mandible
compound eyes
legs
head
thorax
wings
abdomen
stinger

page 2

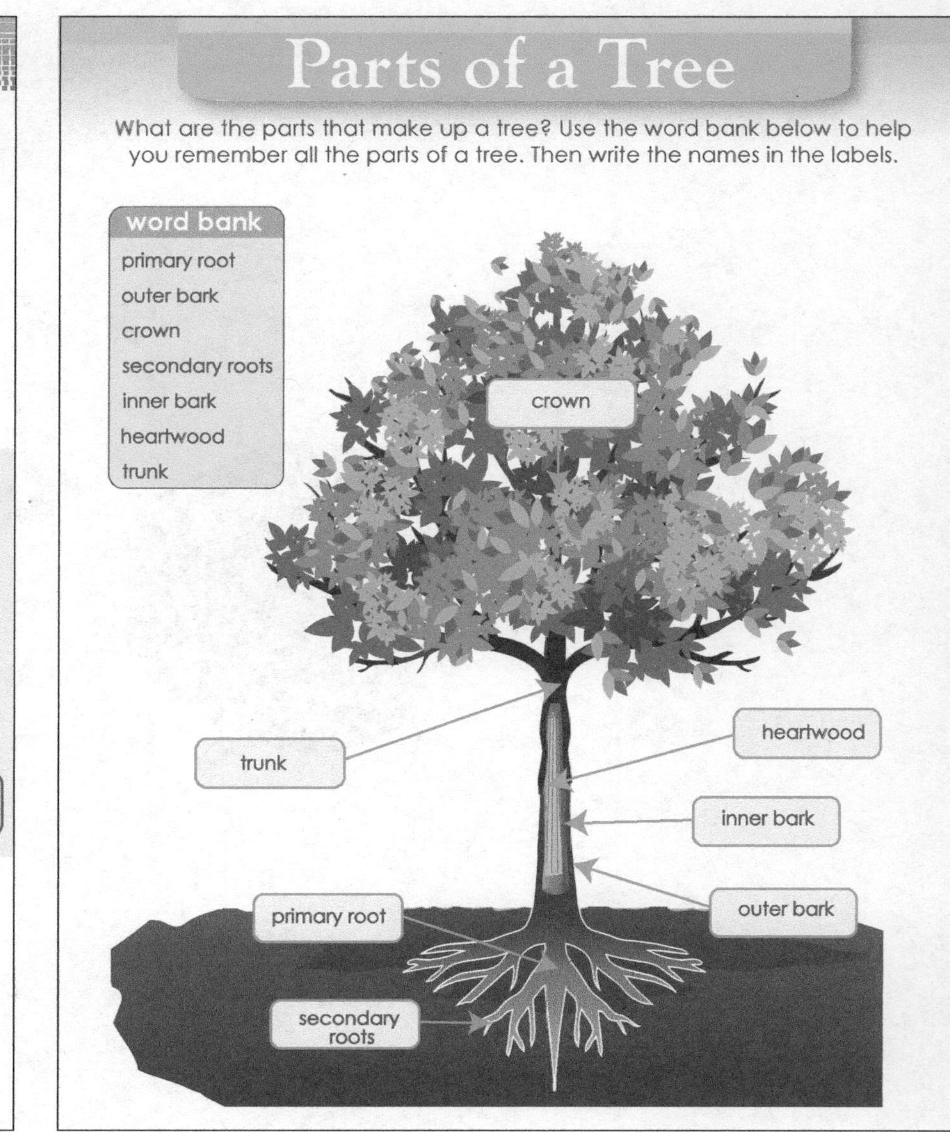
Parts of a Tree
What are the parts that make up a tree? Use the word bank below to help you remember all the parts of a tree. Then write the names in the labels.
word bank
primary root
outer bark
crown
secondary roots
inner bark
heartwood
trunk
crown
trunk
heartwood
inner bark
outer bark
primary root
secondary roots

page 3

Rooms in a House

What are the parts that make up a house? Use the words below to help you remember all the rooms in a house. Then write the names in the labels.

living room | dining room | bathroom | office | kitchen | bedroom | yard

living room
office
bathroom
dining room
bedroom
kitchen
yard

page 8

Parts of a Classroom

What are the parts that make up a classroom? Use the words below to help you remember all the parts in a classroom. Then fill in the labels.

teacher's desk | whiteboard | student's desk | bookcase | computers | chalkboard

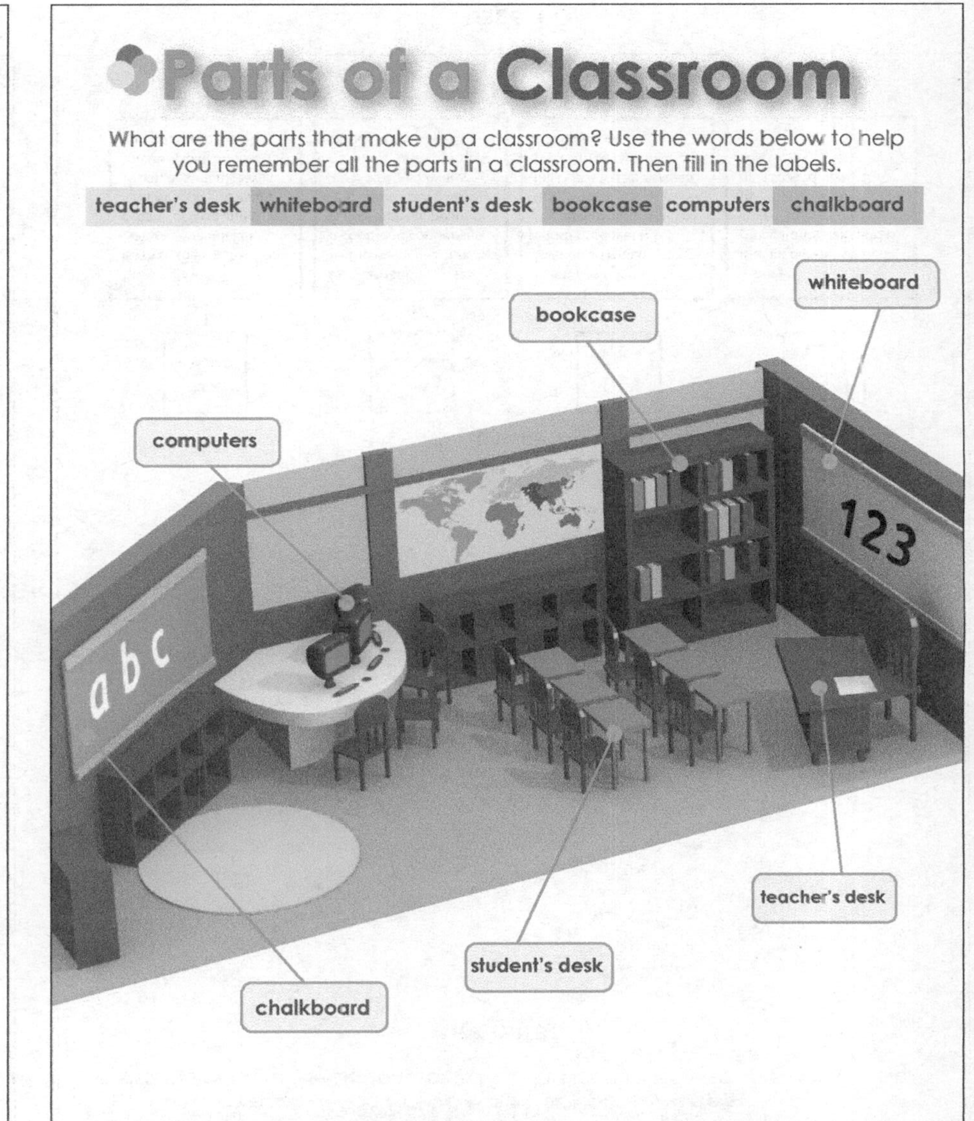

page 9

How Do Clouds Form?

Use the words below and clues at the bottom to fill in the labels that describe how a cloud is formed.

heat cool liquid water rise cloud

Evaporation
takes place as water molecules escape into the air from water, like a puddle, a lake, a stream, or just a droplet of water.

1. heat
2. rise
3. cool
4. liquid water
5. cloud

1. Rays of the sun heat up the moisture in the air close to the ground.
2. As these pockets of air are heated they begin to rise.
3. As these heated pockets of air rise they cool.
4. As it cools, the water vapor turns to tiny droplets of liquid water.
5. The droplets crowd together and form a cloud.

The Water Cycle

Use the clues at the bottom to draw in the icon to finish up the water cycle.

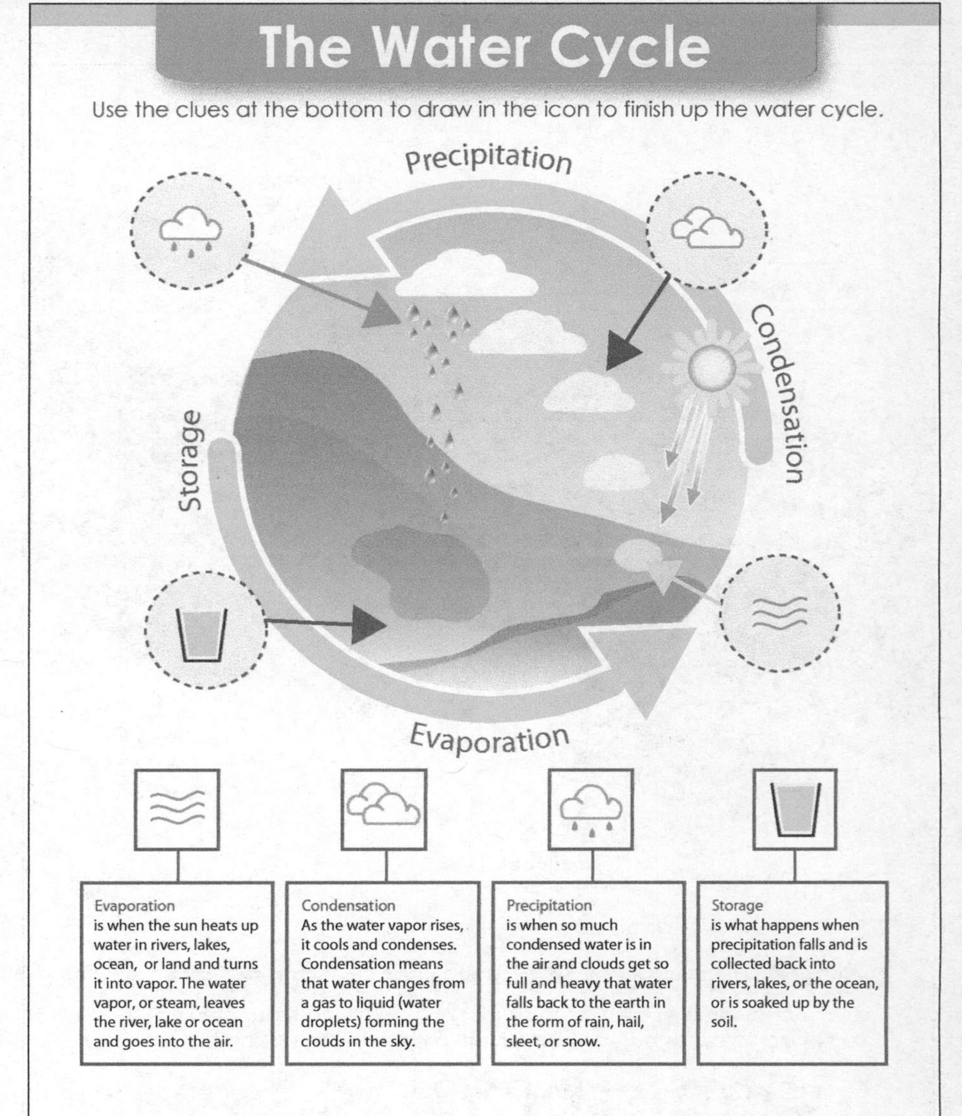

Evaporation	Condensation	Precipitation	Storage
is when the sun heats up water in rivers, lakes, ocean, or land and turns it into vapor. The water vapor, or steam, leaves the river, lake or ocean and goes into the air.	As the water vapor rises, it cools and condenses. Condensation means that water changes from a gas to liquid (water droplets) forming the clouds in the sky.	is when so much condensed water is in the air and clouds get so full and heavy that water falls back to the earth in the form of rain, hail, sleet, or snow.	is what happens when precipitation falls and is collected back into rivers, lakes, or the ocean, or is soaked up by the soil.

Reading a Map

Study the map and use it to answer the questions below.

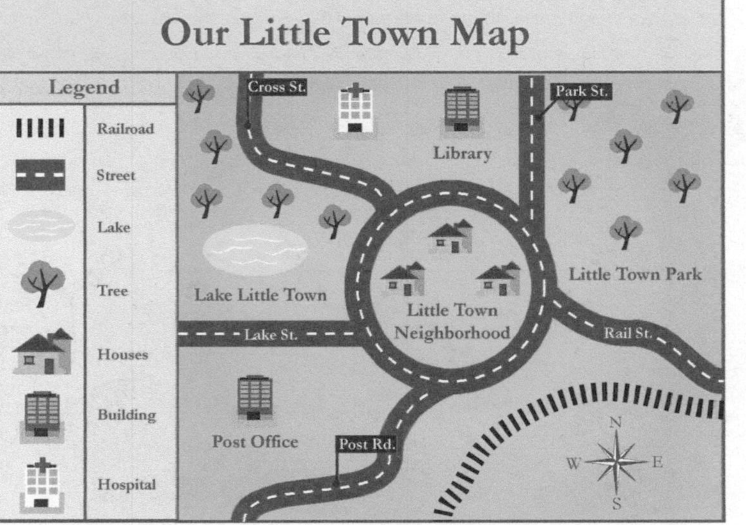

1. What is the title of this map?
   Our Little Town Map
2. From the post office, is the lake north or south?
   North
3. If you are at the library, which direction do you go to get to the town neighborhood?
   South
4. What is west of Little Town Neighborhood?
   Lake Little Town
5. What building is east of the hospital?
   The library

page 18

THE GREAT LAKES

CANADA
Lake Superior
HIGHEST ELEVATION
ST. LAWRENCE RIVER
MINNESOTA
MICHIGAN
Lake Huron
LOWEST ELEVATION
Lake Ontario
NEW YORK
WISCONSIN
Lake Michigan
MICHIGAN
Lake Erie
PENNSYLVANIA
IOWA
ILLINOIS
INDIANA
OHIO
N
W
E
S

1. **LABEL the five Great Lakes and the cardinal directions.**
2. Where are the Great Lakes located in the United States?
   On the northern border, next to Midwest and Northeast states (Answers can vary.)
3. Which Great Lake is completely located in the United States?
   Lake Michigan
4. Which Great Lake is at the highest elevation?
   Lake Superior
5. Which Great Lake is at the lowest elevation?
   Lake Ontario
4. Which of the Great Lakes is farthest west and north?
   Lake Superior
5. Which of the Great Lakes is farthest east?
   Lake Ontario
6. Which river is the primary outlet for the Great Lakes?
   St. Lawrence River
7. Lake Superior is the largest Great Lake. What U.S. States border Lake Superior?
   Minnesota, Michigan, and Wisconsion

page 20

Major U.S. Rivers

Do you know the major rivers of the United States? Use the words below and clues at the bottom to fill in the labels.

Missouri **Mississippi** **Colorado** **Rio Grande** **Hudson** **Ohio**

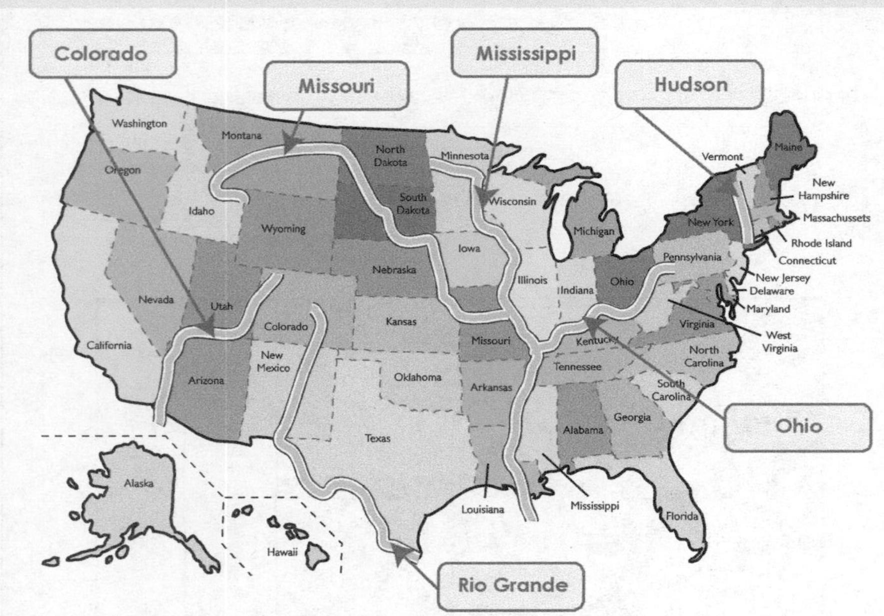

1. This is the major river of the U.S. It flows south from Minnesota and empties into the Gulf of Mexico.
2. This river flows into the Mississippi. It forms part of the borders of Ohio, West Virginia, and more.
3. This river begins in Colorado, flows through New Mexico, and then along the border of Texas.
4. This river begins in Colorado. It moves southwest, ending in the Gulf of California.
5. This river begins in New York, then flows south to form the boundary with New Jersey.
6. This river begins in Montana and flows southeast across the U.S. It ends at the Mississppi River.

page 21

Major U.S. Mountains

Do you know the major mountain ranges of the United States? Use the words below and clues at the bottom to fill in the labels.

Rocky Mountains **Central Appalachians** **Cascade Mountains** **Sierra Nevada Mountains** **Northern Appalachians**

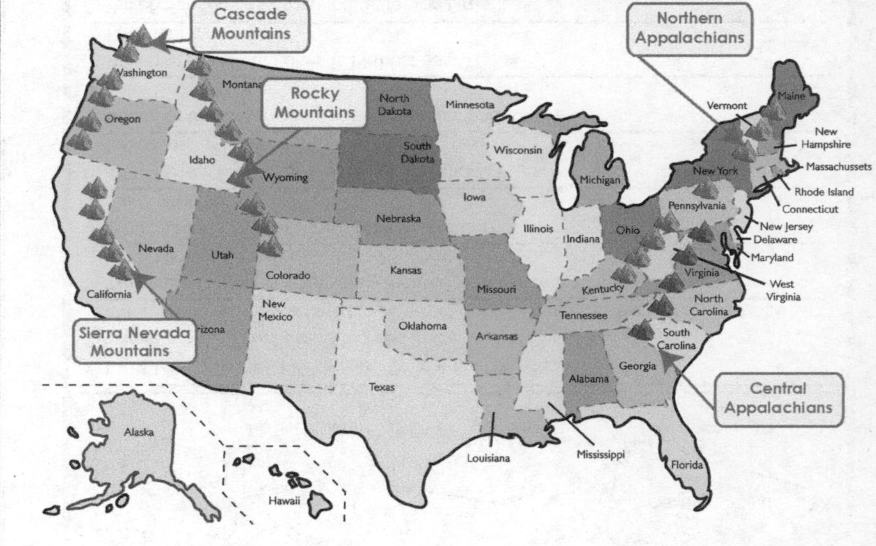

1. These mountains go from Canada to the western U.S. Yellowstone Park is part of this range.
2. This is a sub-section of a larger range; it goes from Canada to the northeastern U.S.
3. This range is full of glaciers and volcanoes, and stretches from Northern California to Canada.
4. This range of snowy mountains is in California and Nevada. Lake Tahoe is in this range.
5. This is a sub-section of a larger range; it goes from Georgia to Pennsylvania.

page 22

RESOURCES

There are 3 main types of Resources. CUT and PASTE the images under the resource they match!

HUMAN RESOURCES are people who use their skills to produce a good or service. (Ex. Teacher)

NATURAL RESOURCES are from nature and are used in their natural form. (Ex. Trees)

CAPITAL RESOURCES are goods produced and used to make other goods or services. (Ex. Buildings, Computers)

CAPITAL RESOURCES	HUMAN RESOURCES	NATURAL RESOURCES
PENCIL	TEACHER	SUN
HAMMER	SCIENTIST	FLOWER
VAN	CHEF	WATER

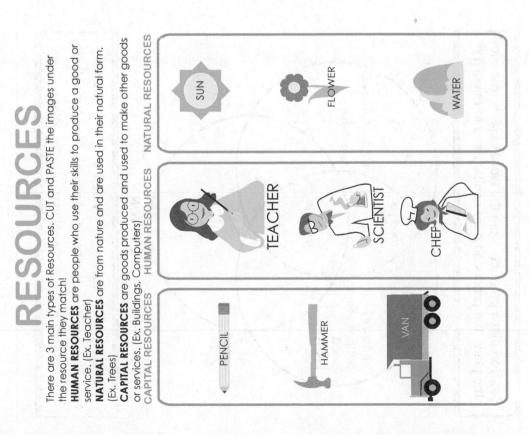

page 26

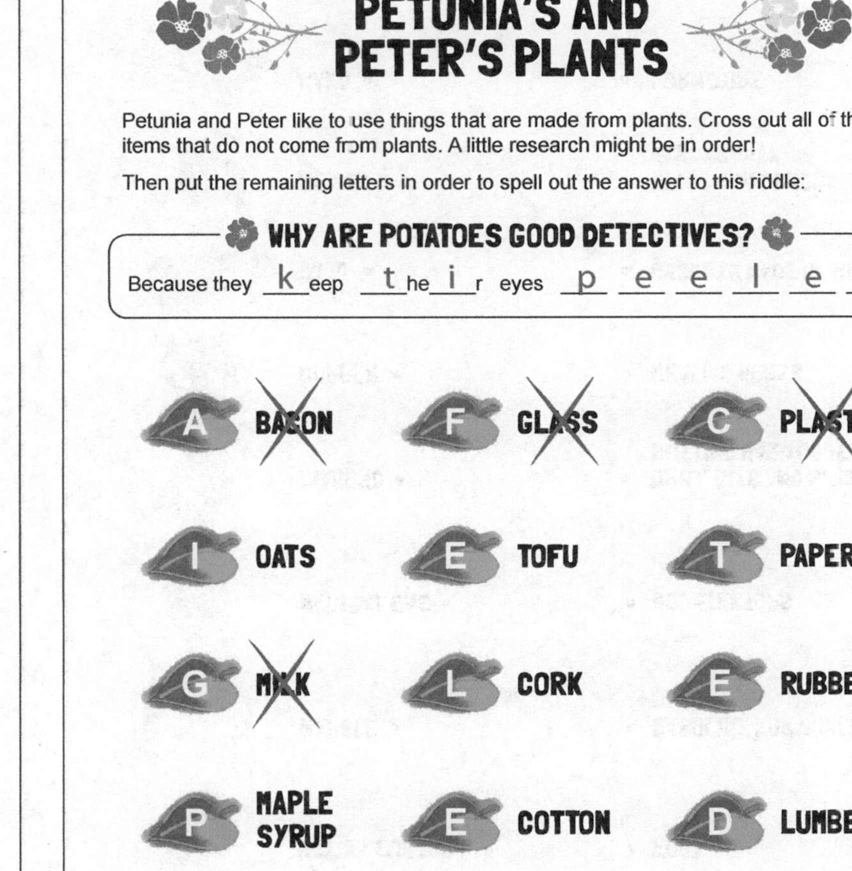

PETUNIA'S AND PETER'S PLANTS

Petunia and Peter like to use things that are made from plants. Cross out all of the items that do not come from plants. A little research might be in order!

Then put the remaining letters in order to spell out the answer to this riddle:

WHY ARE POTATOES GOOD DETECTIVES?

Because they k eep t he i r eyes p e e l e d!

page 32

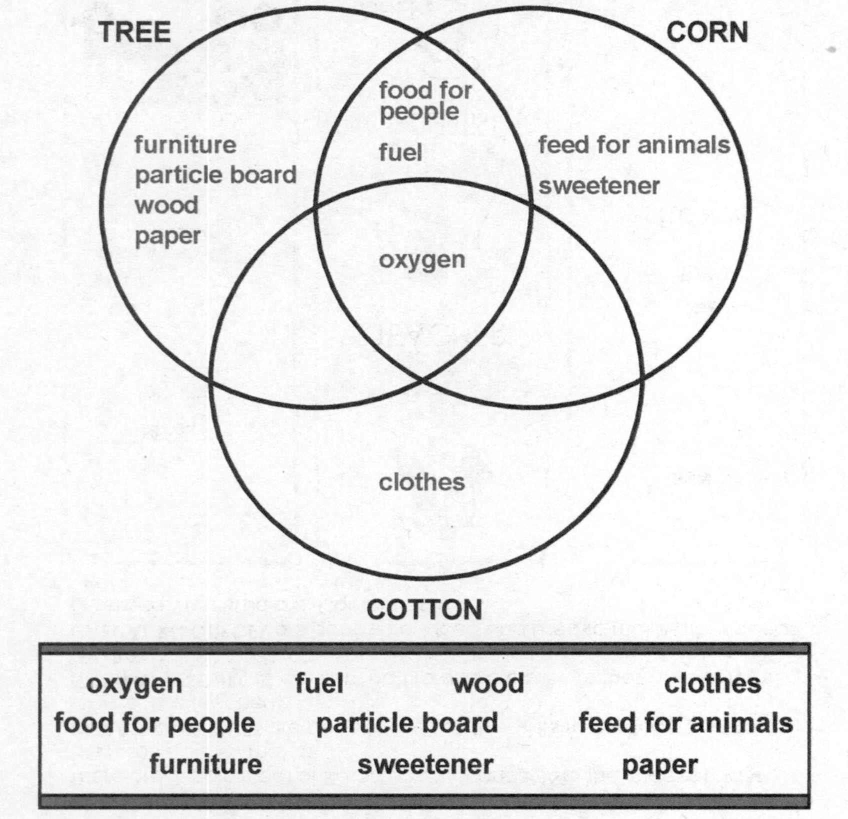
VENN DIAGRAM
Can you place products from the word bank below with the plant that produced it, or can be used to make it?
TREE
CORN
COTTON
furniture
particle board
wood
paper
food for people
fuel
feed for animals
sweetener
oxygen
clothes
oxygen
fuel
wood
clothes
food for people
particle board
feed for animals
furniture
sweetener
paper

page 33

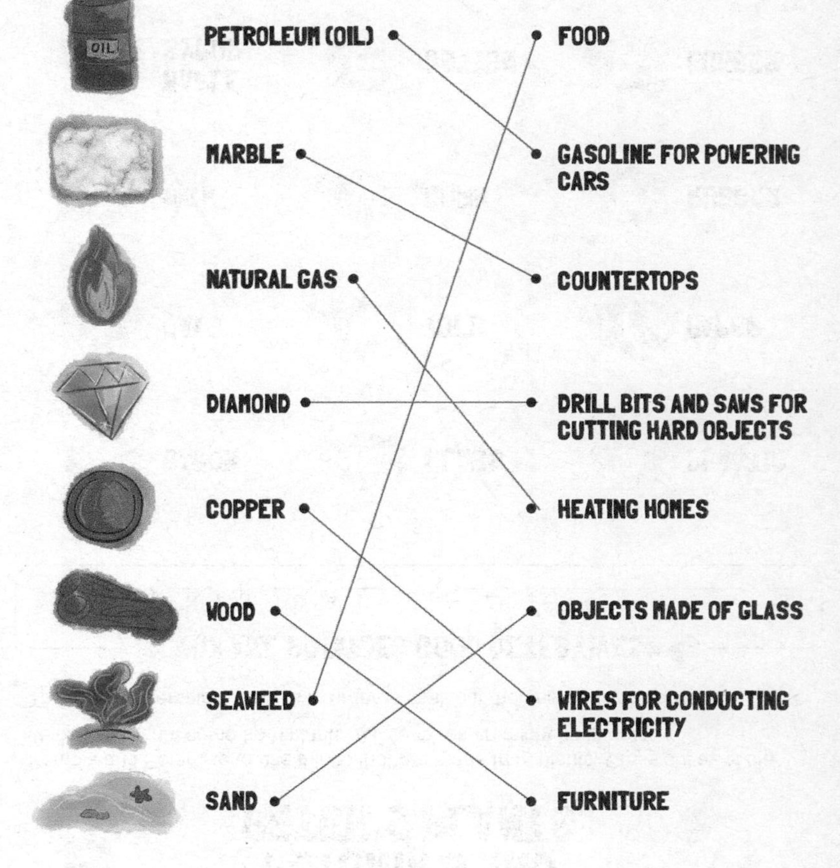
HIDDEN USES: BUILDING RESOURCES VOCABULARY
There are many kinds of natural resources. Some you know well, and some you don't know very well. Below on the left is a list of several natural resources you might not know very much about. On the right is a list of what these resources are used for. Draw a line from the resource on the left to the use of that resource on the right.
OIL
PETROLEUM (OIL)
MARBLE
NATURAL GAS
DIAMOND
COPPER
WOOD
SEAWEED
SAND
FOOD
GASOLINE FOR POWERING CARS
COUNTERTOPS
DRILL BITS AND SAWS FOR CUTTING HARD OBJECTS
HEATING HOMES
OBJECTS MADE OF GLASS
WIRES FOR CONDUCTING ELECTRICITY
FURNITURE

page 35

WHO EATS WHAT?

BUILDING RESOURCES VOCABULARY

Some animals, like tigers, are **carnivores**. That means they eat only meat (which comes from other animals).

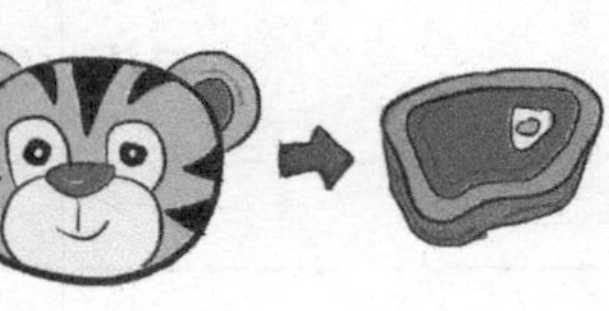
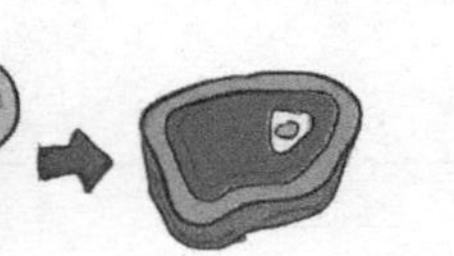
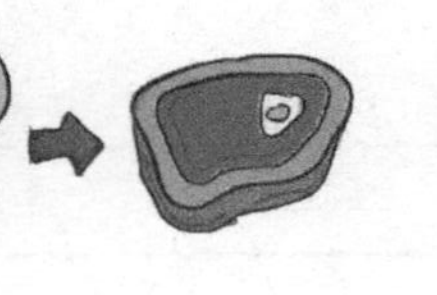

Some animals, like deer, are **herbivores**, which means they eat only plants.

Human beings are called **omnivores**, because we eat plants and meat.

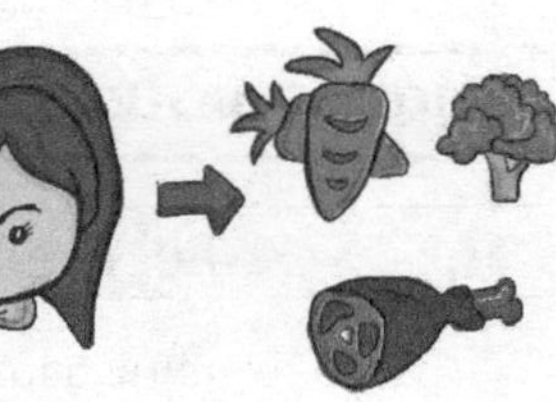
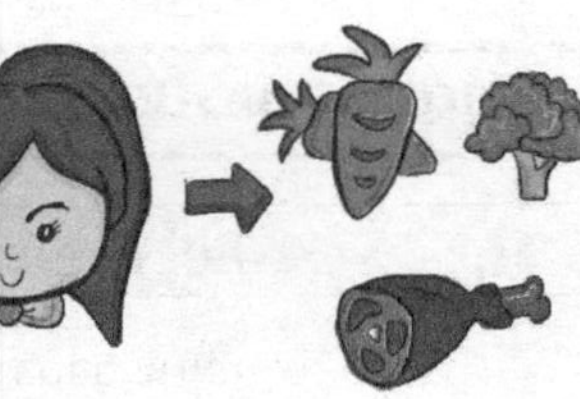
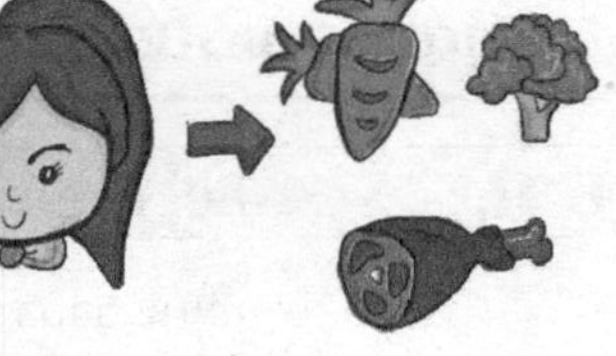

To continue building your resources vocabulary identify the animals below and on the next page as carnivores, herbivores, or omnivores.

HERBIVORES

RABBITS

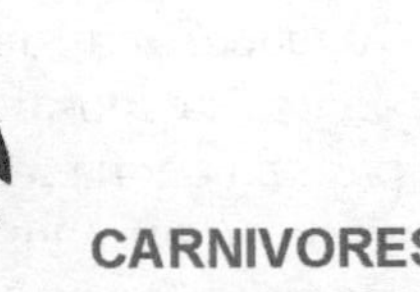

CARNIVORES

EAGLES

HERBIVORES

GIANT PANDAS

OMNIVORES

RACCOONS

CARNIVORES

LEOPARDS

HERBIVORES

COWS

HERBIVORES

HAMSTERS

MOST BEARS ARE OMNIVORES

BEARS

OMNIVORES

COYOTES

CARNIVORES

SNAKES

Natural Resources Mix and Match

Renewable resources are resources that can be replaced in a few years or decades, at about the same rate they are being used. Nonrenewable resources are resources that are being used up faster than they can be replaced. These resources can take anywhere from hundreds to millions of years to regenerate—and in some cases they never will.

Use the chart below to classify each resource as renewable or nonrenewable.

Renewable	Nonrenewable
SUN	NATURAL GAS
WIND	OIL
WATER	
TREES	
AIR	

NATURAL GAS

TREES **AIR** **WATER**

OIL **WIND** **SUN**

page 45

Natural Resources Word Find

Natural resources are non-living things from nature that are used to support life on Earth. Can you find 6 examples of natural resources in the word find below?

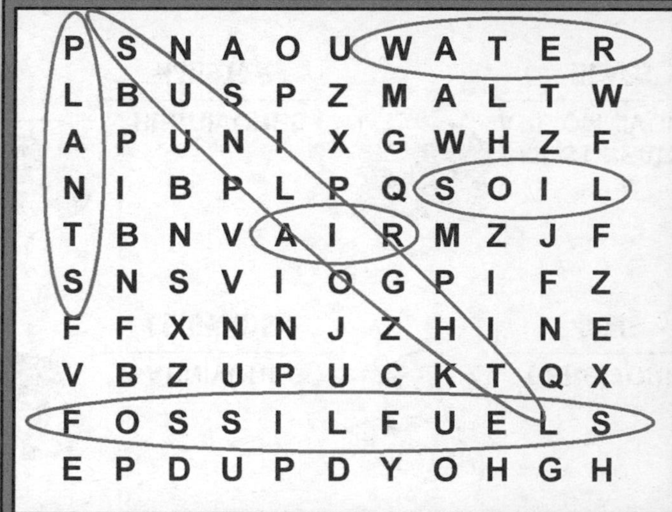

WATER AIR SOIL
PLANTS FOSSIL FUELS SUNLIGHT

page 48

MATCH THE ROCKS

Can you identify the 3 main types of rocks?
Sedimentary, Metamorphic, and Igneous

Draw a line to connect the attribute to the correct rock type.

These rocks have small, shiny, or sparkly crystals.

These rocks have fossils or imprints of leaves, shells, or insects.

Some of these rocks may have holes like swiss cheese.

Some of these rocks are not rough but smooth and shiny like glass.

These rocks have ribbon like layers.

In these rocks you may see individual stones, pebbles, or sand grains.

WEATHERING & EROSION

Weathering is what breaks down rocks and boulders and turns them into tiny pieces called sediment. There are three main types of weathering.

Types of Weathering

Physical Weathering / Mechanical Weathering is when nature plays a part in breaking down big rocks or mountains. There are no chemical changes in this type of weathering. Can you think of 3 types of weather that could break down rocks and soil into smaller parts?

wind, snow, high heat, tornadoes, hurricanes, rain, pressure release (below the earth's surface), tidal waves, salt crystal growth, etc.

Chemical Weathering is when chemical reactions break down big rocks or mountains. Can you think of one example of chemical weathering which happens when gases like nitrogen or sulfur are in the air?

acid rain

Biological Weathering / Organic Weathering is when living things break down big rocks or mountains. This type of weathering is usually a combination of chemical and physical weathering. Can you think of 3 living things that could break down rocks and soil into smaller parts?

bees, ants, earthworms, tree roots, lichens, moss, humans, moles, etc.

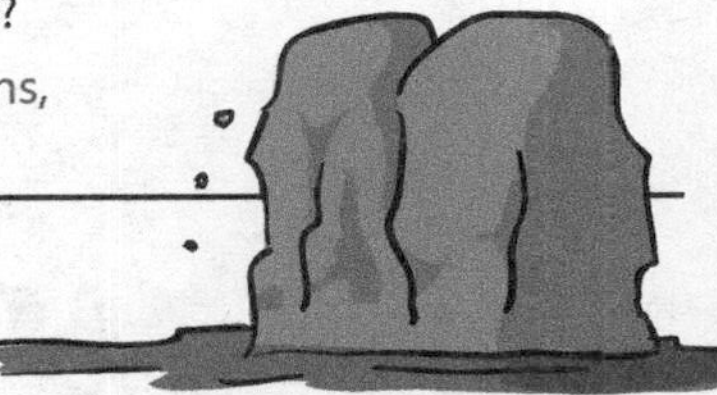

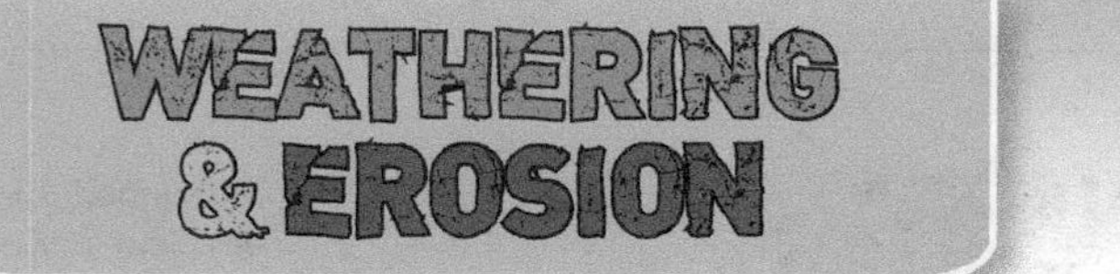

Take a look at the pictures below. Can you tell which type of weathering caused each of these things? Use your knowledge of the different types of weathering to help you make an educated guess. Write your answer under each picture.

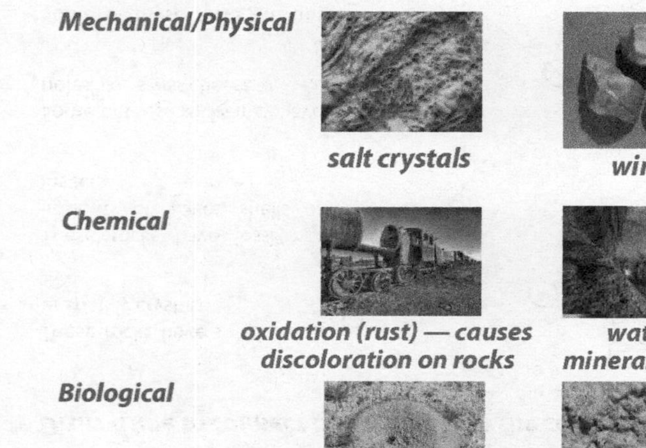

Mechanical/Physical

salt crystals | *wind*

Chemical

oxidation (rust) — causes discoloration on rocks | *water — dissolves minerals and creates caves*

Biological

ants | *bees*

Word Bank

salt crystals	*ants*	*wind*
oxidation (rust)	*Water dissolving minerals*	*bees*

page 58

Types of Soil

Response Questions

Which soil type can become hard as stone when dry? ***Clay***

Which soil type dries out quickly after a rainfall? ***Sand***

Which soil type would be best for building a structure? ***Clay***

Which soil type would a gardener need to break up every now and then to allow more drainage? ***Silt***

Which soil type would a cactus do well in? ***Sand***

TRY THIS!

Dig down at least six inches and grab a handful of soil. Soak it with water and roll it into a ball in your hand.

Sand

Silt

Clay

If you cannot make a ball out of it, it is mostly sand.

If it forms a loose ball but crumbles when squeezed it is mostly silt.

If it forms a packed ball and can be reshaped into a snake, it is mostly clay.

page 62

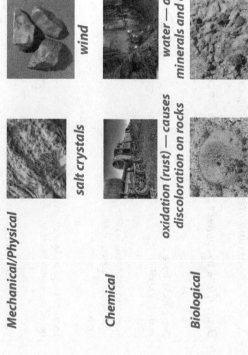

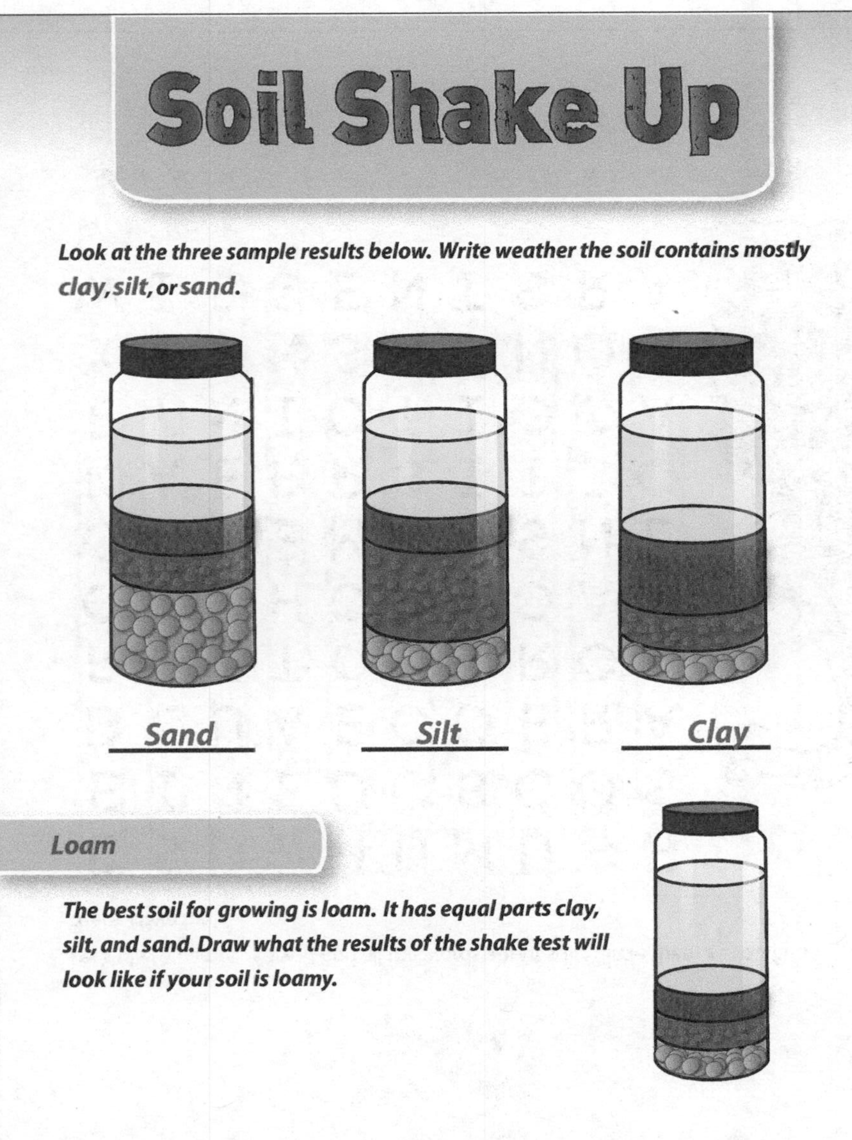

Soil Shake Up
Look at the three sample results below. Write weather the soil contains mostly clay, silt, or sand.
Sand
Silt
Clay
Loam
The best soil for growing is loam. It has equal parts clay, silt, and sand. Draw what the results of the shake test will look like if your soil is loamy.

page 66

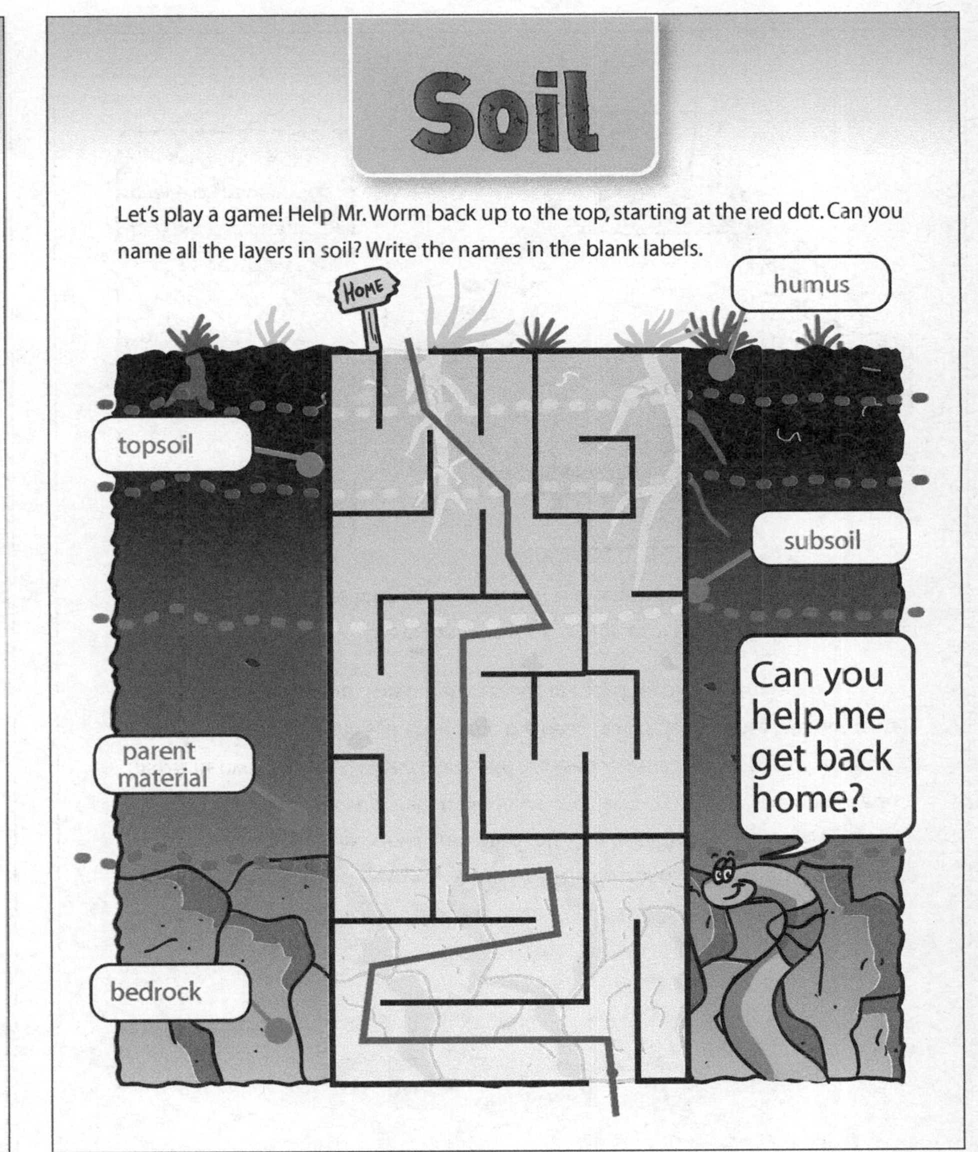

Soil
Let's play a game! Help Mr. Worm back up to the top, starting at the red dot. Can you name all the layers in soil? Write the names in the blank labels.
HOME
humus
topsoil
subsoil
parent material
bedrock
Can you help me get back home?

page 68

Soil

Let's play a game! Can you find all the words about soil? Circle them as you find them. Have fun!

B S D W H U M U S H
E I N E D C S C O S
D L U A E O O E R A
R T T T C M I R G N
O C R H O P L O A D
C L I E M O L S N L
K A E R P S I I I O
E Y N I O T I O C A
X F T N S H D N Q M
W I S G E N T S R A

Word Bank

Sand Silt Clay Loam Soil Compost Nutrients Organic Decompose Humus Bedrock Weathering Erosion

Compost

What is compost?

Compost is ***organic*** material that has been ***decomposed***. Organic material is anything from the earth — fruits, veggies, plants, dirt, and more When organic material decomposes, it breaks down into nutrients that fertilize the soil. Some people make their own compost to help their gardens or farm crops grow, but nature also makes its own compost! When plants die or when leaves fall from trees, they form ***mulch*** that protects the soil. Over time the dead leaves decompose into nutrients that feed the new plants. This is nature's way of recycling old materials.

DRAW THE CYCLE — The compost cycle is a type of life cycle, similar to the water cycle. Fill in the pictures to show each step of the compost cycle.

Organic — natural, living matter
Decomposed — when something is broken down into smaller parts
Mulch — a material, such as dead leaves or bark, spread around or over a plant to enrich or protect the soil

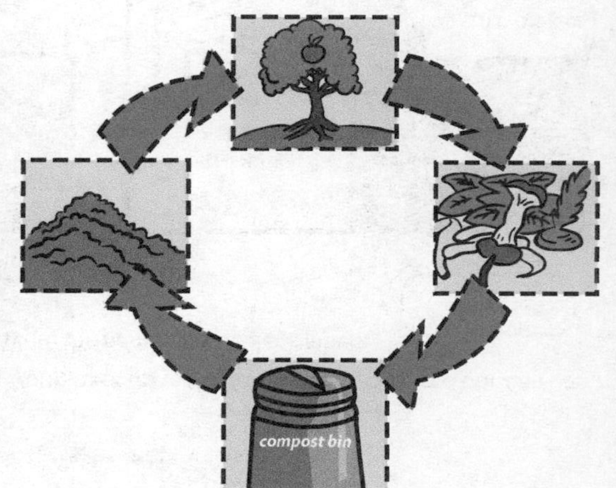

Compost

What is compost?

Compost is organic matter that has been decomposed and recycled as a fertilizer and soil amendment.

What are the 4 main ingredients in the recipe for compost?

*The micro-organisms that recycle leaves and other plant parts need an even mix of **brown stuff and green stuff** to munch on. They also need air and water to live and work. Put all this together and in time you will have compost!*

*Can you think of any items that **should not** be put in your compost?*

Don't use meat, bones, cheese, pet droppings, milk, fats, oils, or diseased plants.

What is "brown stuff" and what is "green stuff"?

*Brown **stuff is dead**, dried plant parts like leaves and pine needles. Green **stuff is** fresh, living parts like grass clippings, kitchen vegetable scraps, weeds, and other plants.*

page 73

Parts of a Tree

Trees have different parts that serve their own special functions. The **primary root** of the tree is the thickest. It holds the plant in the soil and takes in water and nutrients. The **secondary root** branches from the primary root. It helps support the tree, and also takes in water and nutrients from the soil. A tree's **leaves** use light and energy from the sun to make sugar and carbon dioxide to feed the plant. Lastly, the stem or **trunk** keeps distance between the leaves and and the soil while carrying nutrients from the roots to the upper parts of the tree.

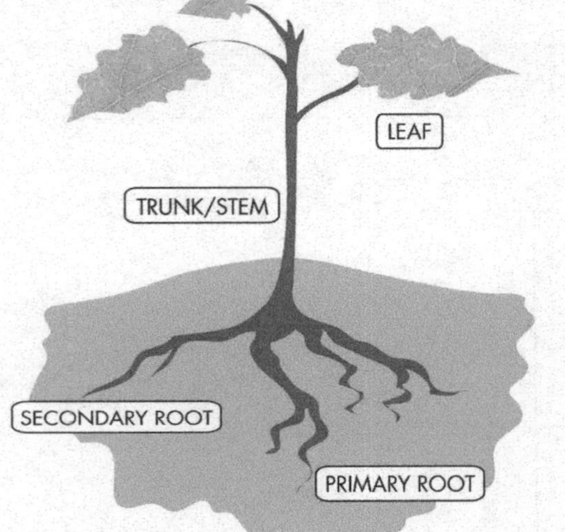

I take in lots of water from the soil and hold the tree firmly in place. I am the...

PRIMARY ROOT .

I keep distance between the leaves and the soil, while delivering food. I am the...

TRUNK .

I use light and heat to make food for the rest of the tree. I am the...

LEAF .

I assist the larger root in supporting the tree, as well as taking in water. I am the...

SECONDARY ROOT .

page 80

TREE SCRAMBLE

Unscramble the letters to reveal parts of a tree. You can experiment with different words from the box below.

UFRTI
F R U I T

VEASLE
L E A V E S

RABHCN
B R A N C H

UKNTR
T R U N K

OOSRT
R O O T S

BRANCH	LEAVES	STUMP	GRASS
FRUIT	NEEDLES	TALL	NEST
THORN	ROOTS	GREEN	TRUNK

page 82

TREE MÈASURING

Use a ruler to measure this tree. First, write down your estimate of the length to the nearest inch and centimeter. Then, use a ruler to perform a more accurate measurement, again rounding to the nearest inch or centimeter.

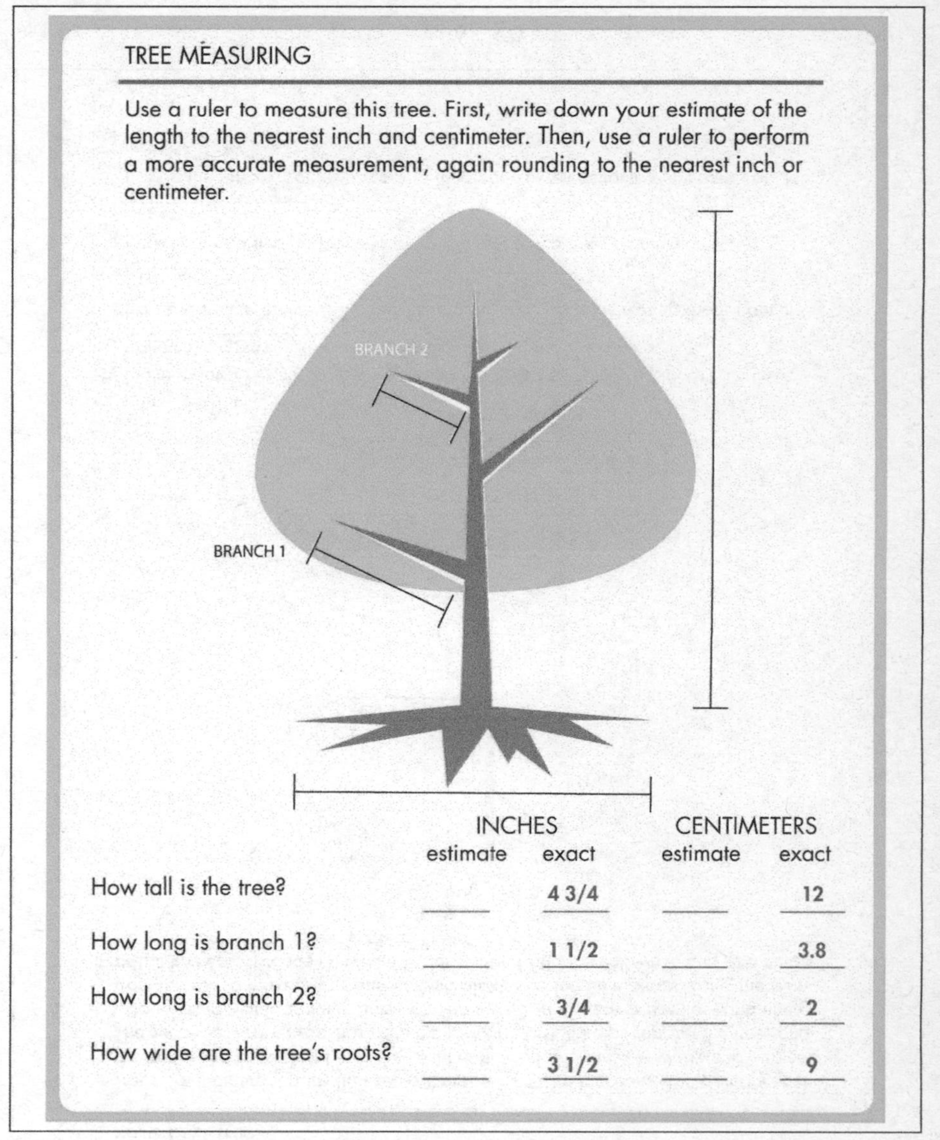

	INCHES		CENTIMETERS	
	estimate	exact	estimate	exact
How tall is the tree?	____	4 3/4	____	12
How long is branch 1?	____	1 1/2	____	3.8
How long is branch 2?	____	3/4	____	2
How wide are the tree's roots?	____	3 1/2	____	9

page 83

GROWING TREES

Trees are important natural resources. Find out how many trees Bobby planted in the past few weeks by reading the pictograph below. Then, answer the questions.

Note: each tree in the pictograph stands for 2 trees.

WEEK	NUMBER OF TREES
WEEK 1	
WEEK 2	
WEEK 3	
WEEK 4	
WEEK 5	

= 2 trees

1. What does this symbol represent?
THIS SYMBOL REPRESENTS ONE TREE.
2. How many trees did Bobby plant in week 3?
BOBBY PLANTED 13 TREES IN WEEK 3.
3. In which week did Bobby plant the fewest trees? How many did he plant that week?
BOBBY PLANTED THE FEWEST TREES IN WEEK 1. HE PLANTED 6 TREES THAT WEEK.
4. In which week did Bobby plant the most trees? How many more did he plant in that week than in week 1?
BOBBY PLANTED THE MOST TREES IN WEEK 2. HE PLANTED 14 TREES THAT WEEK.
5. Draw symbols to represent 5 trees.

page 84

How Do Apples Grow?
Some apple trees will grow over 40 feet high and live over 100 years!
CUT OUT THE PEICES AND PASTE THEM IN ORDER OF GROWTH

page 87

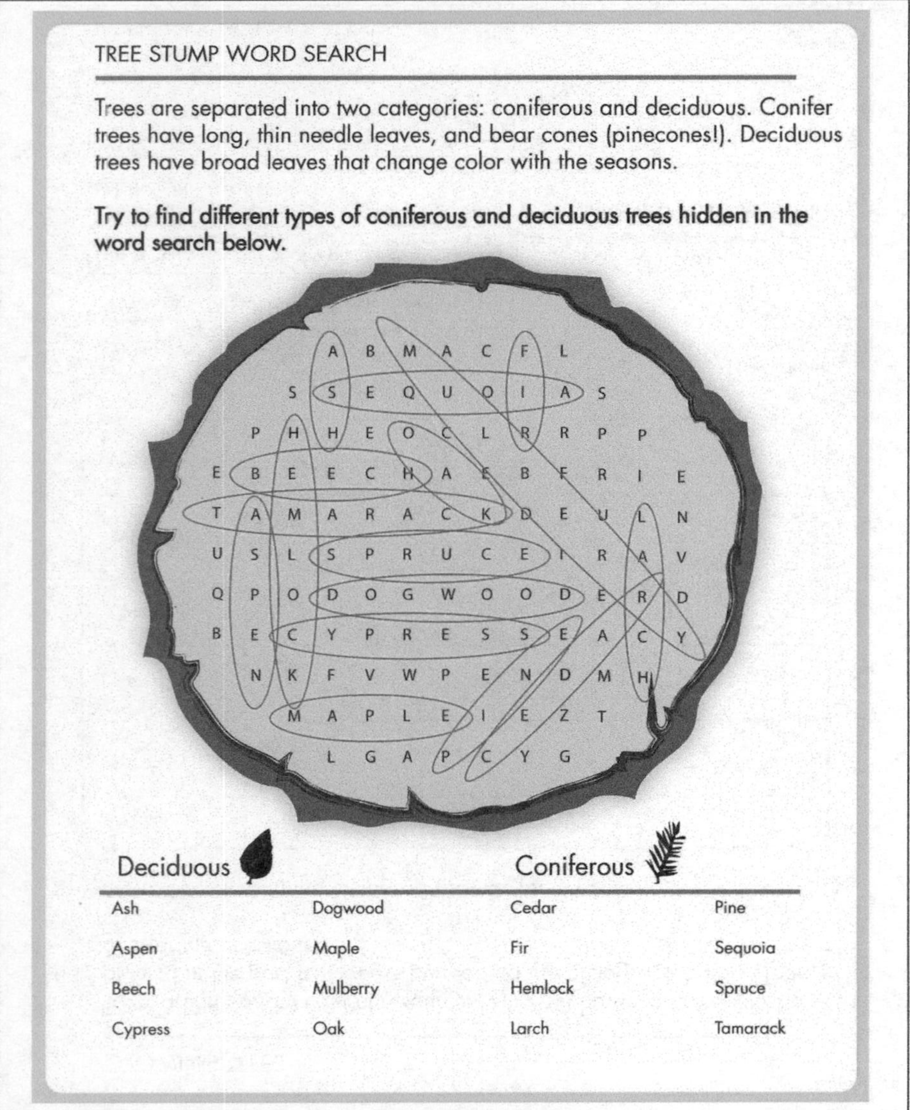

TREE STUMP WORD SEARCH

Trees are separated into two categories: coniferous and deciduous. Conifer trees have long, thin needle leaves, and bear cones (pinecones!). Deciduous trees have broad leaves that change color with the seasons.

Try to find different types of coniferous and deciduous trees hidden in the word search below.

Deciduous		Coniferous	
Ash	Dogwood	Cedar	Pine
Aspen	Maple	Fir	Sequoia
Beech	Mulberry	Hemlock	Spruce
Cypress	Oak	Larch	Tamarack

page 93

TREE CLIMBERS

The animals listed on the tree are all good climbers. Can you find them in the word search below?

page 96

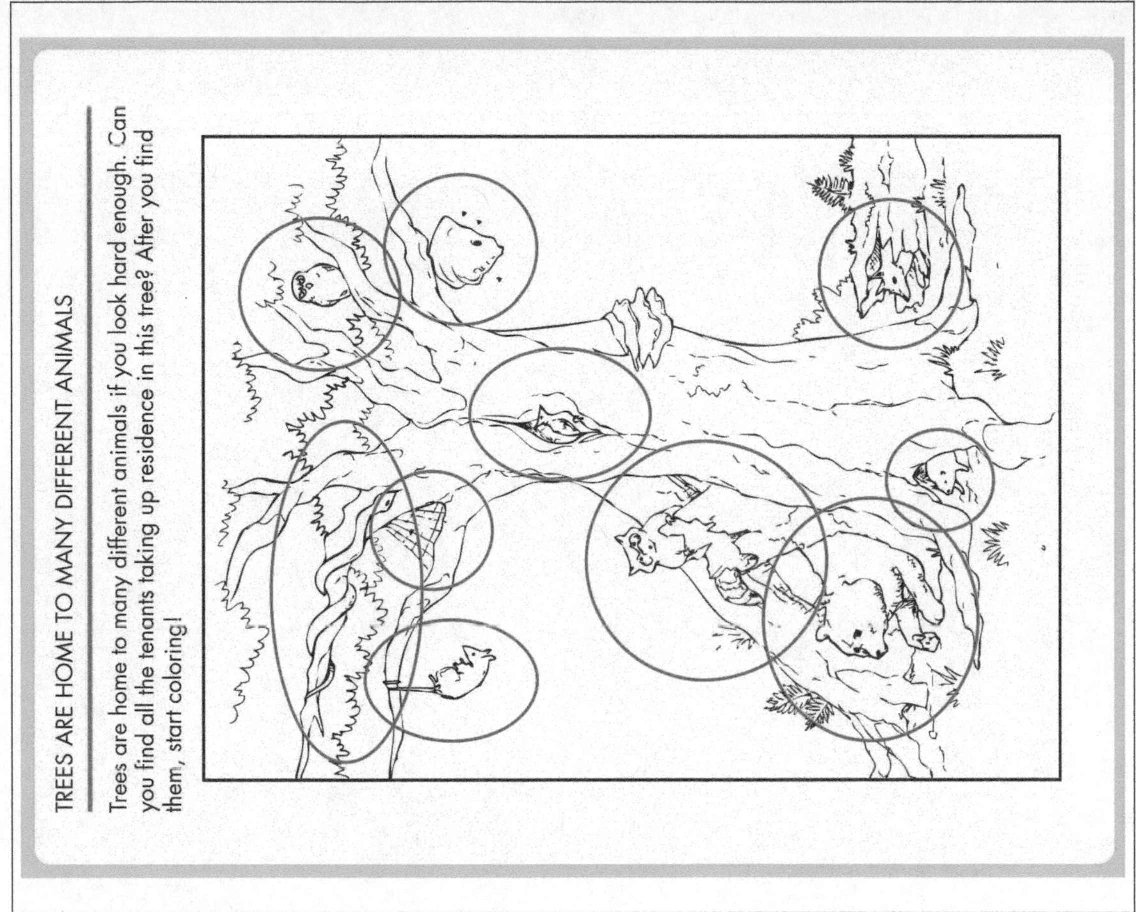

TREES ARE HOME TO MANY DIFFERENT ANIMALS

Trees are home to many different animals if you look hard enough. Can you find all the tenants taking up residence in this tree? After you find them, start coloring!

page 99

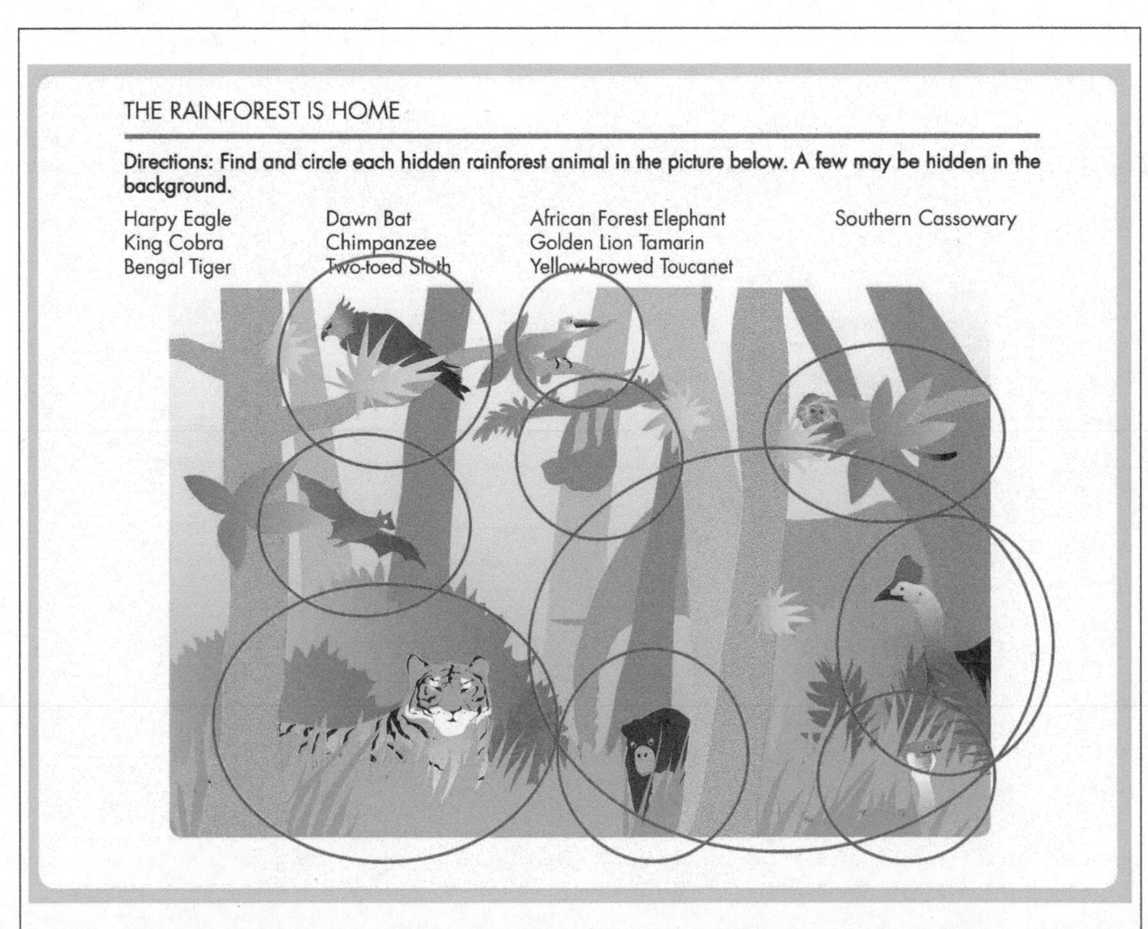

THE RAINFOREST IS HOME

Directions: Find and circle each hidden rainforest animal in the picture below. A few may be hidden in the background.

Harpy Eagle
King Cobra
Bengal Tiger
Dawn Bat
Chimpanzee
Two-toed Sloth
African Forest Elephant
Golden Lion Tamarin
Yellow-browed Toucanet
Southern Cassowary

page 98